Gifted at Risk:
Poetic Portraits

Jean Sunde Peterson, Ph.D.

Great Potential Press®
Scottsdale, Arizona
www.giftedbooks.com

Gifted at Risk: Poetic Portraits

Edited by: Jennifer Ault
Interior Design: The Printed Page
Cover Design: Hutchison-Frey

Published by Great Potential Press, Inc.
P.O. Box 5057
Scottsdale, AZ 85261

13 12 11 10 09   5 4 3 2 1

At the time of this book's publication, all facts and figures cited are the most current available. All telephone numbers, addresses, and website URLs are accurate and active; all publications, organizations, websites, and other resources exist as described in this book; and all have been verified as of the time this book went to press. The author(s) and Great Potential Press make no warranty or guarantee concerning the information and materials given out by organizations or content found at websites, and we are not responsible for any changes that occur after this book's publication. If you find an error or believe that a resource listed here is not as described, please contact Great Potential Press.

Library of Congress Cataloging-in-Publication Data

Peterson, Jean Sunde, 1941-
 Gifted at risk : poetic portraits / Jean Sunde Peterson.
   p. cm.
 Includes index.
 ISBN 978-0-910707-97-8
 1. Gifted children—Education. 2. Underachievers—Education. I. Title.
 LC3993.P47 2009
 371.95—dc22
     2009032516

Dedication

This book is dedicated to the exceptional, memorable, and wonderfully complex individuals who are introduced in this volume so that they can continue instructing.

Contents

Acknowledgments vii

Preface ix

Introduction 1

Gifted 4

Not a Good Fit 6

Caught Off Guard 8

High Achiever 10

The Recommendation 12

Spoiled 14

Cause and Effect 16

A Memorable Experience 18

The Writing on the Wall 20

In the Resistance 22

From A to Z 24

Eating Disorder 26

Victim 28

The Writer 30

The Parent 32

Three Boys 34

Goosebumps 36

Warm Eyes 38

To Hear Better 40

Eighth Grader 42

He Has Edges 44

Hunk 46

Common Denominators 48

Persistence 50

He Couldn't Wait 52

Poor Speller 54

Sweaty 56

The Credit 58

Yearbook Photographer 60

Only by Grace 62

About Junior High 64

Trying to Fix Himself 66

When the Advocate Died 68
Wounded 70
Brian and Christi 72
The Nicest Girl in School 74
Guilty 76
Underachievers 78
Achievers 80
Presentation by Dr. A 82
Bonsai Tree 84
Awake at Night 86
Broken Yardstick 88
When Kennedy Died 90
Revenge of the Nerds 92
Whatever 94
Explanation 96
Mentor Teacher 98
Laughing about the Letter 100
A Teacher Running 102
A Place with Color 104
Seven-Year-Old 106
Grief in the Queue 108
Way Off the Charts 110
Surprised 112
Prisoner of Love 114
Sasha and I 116
At the Workshop 118
Optimal Range 120
Small-Town Principal 122
Their Gift 124
Sad Boy 126
Many Kinds 128
Index by Theme 131
About the Author 134

Acknowledgments

I remain grateful to Fred Stephens, principal of the high school where I began my group work with high-ability students. He made sure we had a private, comfortable place to meet, and he understood the value of the discussion groups. Penny Oldfather, district coordinator of gifted education, had recruited me, and she offered unconditional support for developing a complex program.

Without the components that were intended to support social and emotional development, and without access to the kids' subjective experience of it, I would not have added a passion to my second career in education. Passion generates energy for exploration beyond the ordinary and the expected, and there's nothing mundane about working with gifted kids.

My experiences with the individuals and groups portrayed in the poems here, and with many others as well, have been catalytic in my professional and personal development.

Preface

Just before I left many years in K-12 education to prepare for my new career as a counselor educator, one of the graduating seniors presented me with a thank-you gift—a journal with 20 blank lines on each of its 365 pages. She said, "You probably have a lot to write about." Sara knew I had organized, in the program I directed, a "breakfast club" for poets. At weekly meetings, while they ate, they shared what they had written during the week and also wrote prompt-generated poetry. I wrote with them. Mostly academic under-achievers, these students often "left me in their dust" with their amazing work.

Each page of the lovely new journal had an ornate border and begged for a pithy poem. For the next year, on most days, I wrote one. There were portraits of complex and highly capable students, both past and present; images from my rural childhood; and mid-life perspectives. When the year ended, I real-ized that I had more than 80 poems in the student portrait category. Sometimes, when I spoke to teachers and parents during the next few years, I included one of the poems to make a point about social and emotional devel-opment of gifted kids. These days, I use the poems routinely and am often asked if they are available. Now they are.

As an English teacher, reflecting my preferred modes, I favored a constructivist approach to teaching: open-ended writing assignments with general parameters, journal responses to readings, personalized learning, and speakers to provide context for assigned novels. The summer foreign language day camps I directed embraced varied learning styles and encouraged creativ-ity in the teachers.

Counseling practice and educating counselors are only short leaps from what especially interested me in literature, in students' writing, and in summer work: human development. Counselors need to learn to tolerate ambiguity and lack of closure, to be nonjudgmental, and to enter the world of clients and be taught by them. I have tried to model that for my graduate students as we engage in mutual learning. This professional posture has long allowed me to participate in the development of gifted children, adolescents, and young adults. I continue to learn how they think and feel through what and how they communicate.

The high school gifted education program I directed had 25 program options, many of them comfortable for highly able students who resisted more-and-faster options. Community volunteers led after-school or lunch-hour components like mime, dance, philosophy, classical music appreciation, and creative writing. Weekly after-school lectures on topics that were not part of the school curriculum attracted up to 80 students and teachers, with teachers sometimes giving extra credit for attendance. Students gathered to study unusual languages after school. Art competitions, inter-school/inter-state/national group competitions, opportunities to teach foreign languages weekly in elementary schools, and brief career shadowing all generated considerable interest and participation.

However, weekly discussion groups focusing on social and emotional development were the most popular option by far. Approximately 115 gifted achievers and underachievers attended them for the entire year, continuing until they graduated. Group size was 7-10 students. Those meetings, each with a specific focus, gave both high achieving and underachieving gifted students a nonjudgmental, non-evaluative environment to make non-academic connections with each other. They shared experiences related to "growing up." They discovered common interests, explored concerns, felt affirmed, and expressed sensitivities, passions, doubts, and vulnerabilities. Simultaneously, they taught me, of course, though I did not think in those terms at the time. Individually and collectively, their complexity defied common one-dimensional stereotypes of gifted students, and they were certainly more than just performers or non-performers, computer geeks, skateboarders, athletes, musicians, artists, or student leaders.

Later, I came to appreciate that I had had a rare vantage point for observing the social and emotional development of gifted teens, and I chose to continue that focus in qualitative and sometimes longitudinal research in my university teaching career. The hundreds of gifted students I became acquainted with during 19 years of classroom teaching, 15 years of day camps, nine years of clinical work, and six years of gifted education small-group work in schools continue to help me prepare counselors to differentiate services for kids like them. The same is true when I speak to teachers and parents about social and emotional development of gifted kids. The individuals who inspired the poems in this book are often in my thoughts. Sara's gift gave me a nudge to reflect on kids like her—so that I could take them with me.

Introduction

It is important that teachers in both regular and self-contained classrooms, program coordinators, school administrators, classroom peers, and the public at large be aware that gifted individuals do not lead charmed lives, even though it might appear that most who fit common stereotypes do have advantages even beyond ability. However, in one 10-year longitudinal study that I conducted about events in the lives of gifted graduating seniors (almost all fitting the high-achieving stereotype), 94 immediate/extended family deaths had occurred for the 105 who had persisted in the study to that point, in addition to 77 serious illnesses in immediate and extended family, 17 major changes in family constellation, 15 chronic illnesses in the students themselves, 10 deaths of friends, and eight serious car accidents. Additionally, three parental or teacher incarcerations were reported.

When they graduated, the student participants wrote about how negative events had changed their lives—one noting that the struggles changed him in positive ways, others commenting about learning to adjust after major impact, and still others mentioning a changed worldview or loss of trust. Some seniors, whose parents had reported major tragedies in their annual reports, did not respond themselves at graduation, leaving me wondering how they had fared. Of the 48 who did complete the study at graduation by providing narrative responses to open-ended questions, 47 reported high stress related to academics, 22 reported stressful school and personal transitions, 21 mentioned difficult college decisions, 19 noted problems with peers, and 15 said that heavy extracurricular involvement was the biggest stressor. Some included comments about how they had coped. In general, a theme of resilience emerged amid the recollected challenges.

I continue to be interested in whether and how giftedness is both asset (a potential factor of resilience) and vulnerability (sensitive and potentially intense responses to troubling contexts and experiences). Almost all of the poems in this volume reflect at least one aspect of that asset-burden paradox. I hope that these portraits will provoke productive self-reflection in adults who have significant roles in the lives of gifted youth. I trust that the narrative information related to social and emotional development will also be helpful. Some of my comments are based on clinical and empirical literature. Some of it simply offers further context for a poem. Whether this book finds a home on a coffee table, in a study area, in a college residence hall, in a teacher education syllabus, in a course for counselors or psychologists, in a physician's office, or on a psychiatrist's resource shelf, the individuals in the portraits will continue to raise awareness.

I have taught in five states and in one foreign country, and I have done counseling of various kinds and durations in three states, five cities, 13 schools, and six mental health agencies. The portraits therefore represent a wide variety of locations and venues. When names are used in poems, they are pseudonyms. When a story is presented, it is intended to represent some aspect of risk or characteristic associated with giftedness, and some details have been altered. I present the portraits respectfully, for I hold the subjects in high regard.

Gifted at Risk:
Poetic Portraits

Gifted

We disagree about cut-off
and when the meal should be served
and how to speak when serving it,
whether we should offer dessert
as reward for what they do
with what they have,
or serve entrees and dinner music
as sustenance and nurturance
to keep them alive and well.

We recognize some easily,
of those we should invite to eat,
some not,
these last so apt
to get resistance
from those who have defined them
as unworthy,
the needs of both
and all
not always apparent.

They do not always tell us
who they are,
might not know
what the hunger is,
and do not know
how to ask
for what they need,
for they do not lean
easily or well.

Gifted

As a teacher, I observed some resistance to implementing gifted programs at all school levels. Some educators grappled with the word *gifted* as it moved into the school vocabulary. "All kids are gifted," I'd hear. I'd comment that all kids are indeed unique and special and do have strengths—gifts, if you will. But the kids whose intellectual ability puts them in the top percentiles are as different from the average as kids are in that small range at the other end of the ability scale. They need special services, differentiated to match their social, emotional, career, and cognitive needs. In fact, *giftedness* is often defined as ability that is at least two standard deviations above the mean, and the "tail" on the bell curve of intellectual ability extends far beyond that. Level of difference, and of need, varies accordingly.

In one high school, I encountered hostility in some teachers who wouldn't accept that academic underachievers had a right to be included in a gifted program. One said, testily, "He's getting a D in algebra! What's he doing in that gifted group?" Some wondered how I justified the non-academic small-group work for gifted kids. One argued against the idea of after-school lectures, saying, "No one will come." After observing a group discussing "what I wish teachers understood about kids like me," a principal said, "*All* students should have this opportunity." I said I agreed with him but that my responsibility was to the kids in the program. As an English teacher in other schools, I had become aware of complex concerns, and in the new discussion groups, I could already see that gifted kids appreciated that the program paid attention to social and emotional development.

Later, in several of my studies, I found that highly able students often do not ask for help, even when in great distress. As a teacher and counselor of gifted kids, I also discovered that they need and want psychoeducational information *about* high ability. Sometimes their feelings and thoughts feel "crazy" to them. Too often, they assume that adults in their lives cannot understand their concerns and would be disappointed and unsettled by those feelings and thoughts.

Some parents advocate earnestly for services. Some do not advocate at all. They trust that the school will discover their children's strengths without parental input, they don't understand the available services, or they don't feel comfortable approaching administrators or teachers. To be effective advocates, educators and parents need not only to be informed about gifted education issues, but also to be sensitive to the concerns of all players in the system. Pertinent information needs to be given to advocates, policy-makers, and gifted kids themselves.

Not a Good Fit

I did not know
that men in his family
had a tradition,
so the decision
of this shaggy dreamer,
who never wrote clichés,
to study engineering
took me by surprise.
The invitation
four years later
to his exhibition
of poetic photography
didn't.

He said
that when they checked him off
for millimetric errors,
he knew he didn't care enough—
affirmed the rhythm
of the mold
that was not theirs,
that was broken
long before
day one.

Not a Good Fit

"Fit" in a career is more than doing what one is good at. Personality type matters, whether a person needs closure at the end of the work day or not, prefers being around people to working alone, enjoys working outside instead of inside, thrives on variety and action or needs quiet time for contemplation, has a high tolerance for ambiguity instead of preferring certainty and resolution, likes order in the workday instead of "fragmentation," likes to write or likes to count, enjoys or dislikes bringing details into order, likes to follow instead of lead, prefers staying in one place instead of traveling, wants freedom to be creative or not. People are not usually "one or the other," but all of these aspects of the work world and personality matter when considering a good fit.

"Fit" is also about being involved with something that is interesting. Someone might be good at something but not greatly interested in it for the long haul. Might a strong interest and talent lead to a significant avocation instead of vocation? Values also matter. Is attaining wealth a priority? Does a 70-hour work week mesh well with the lifestyle dream? How much are health and fitness a concern? Immediate and extended family? Protection of natural resources and the environment?

This exceptional young man followed his male relatives' interests when he began working toward an engineering degree. He decided it wasn't a good fit. He felt fortunate to figure that out early in college.

Caught Off Guard

He is a smiling,
handsome,
lean 4.0,
number one
in his large class,
and his drive
is from within,
and that is probably good,
he says,
and he is best
at things he tries—
needs to be,
he says—
and his girl
and parents
are so good,
he says.

He has learned
to talk more,
he says.

Being a student
is not a happy thing,
he says.
He finally asks
if maybe
things might change,
and he might lose
the push.

The question
catches me
off guard—
him, too,
maybe.

Caught Off Guard

I remember this gentle young man's earnestness more than anything else as he sat with me, going over his interest, personality, and values assessments. He and his peers had come to the university for a day of career development activities. What struck me was his insight that everything doesn't always stay the same. He wondered about being able to sustain his motivation to achieve, recognizing that it came from him, not from others. Perhaps he also had some anxiety about being able to continue to meet the expectations that he had generated in people he cared about. He allowed himself to be vulnerable when he indicated that excelling academically was stressful for him.

I wrote this poem to capture the sobering and thought-provoking insight of this serious and self-reflective high school senior. High academic performance during high school is no guarantee of sustained success before the K-12 years end or for scholastic excellence later. One of my own research studies found that one in three students whose grade point at graduation reflected achievement had underachieved at some point during junior and senior high school. In addition, one in five of all achievers performed less well academically in college, and roughly one in 10 *high* achievers actually underachieved during college. Nevertheless, in general, level of achievement was fairly stable from high school to college. Some high achievers experienced depression, relationship break-ups, deaths in the immediate or extended family, unexpected academic challenges, or major adjustments to large city environments and residence hall living. But for many of these achievers, academic performance was unaffected. "Habits of achievement," in my opinion, tend to support high achievers when life circumstances are challenging.

The boy in this poem probably continued to achieve in college. It is even possible that college was less stressful for him than high school had been. If distressing life events interfered, perhaps his long-standing mode of achievement continued to sustain him. If not, then I hope he felt comfortable seeking counseling on campus or informal assistance from other university resources. Based on the fact that he was able to express his concern that day, he could likely do it again when needed and appropriate.

High Achiever

I am amazed at her
    tense
    intensity,
    pressured
    competitiveness,
    rapidity,
    verbosity,
    busyness,
    achievement.
She is scheduled to the minute—
    exotic languages and logic courses
    and music in the evenings.
She giggles
(misses the glances)
and claims her
huge ego is genetic,
brags and
complains
    how everyone comes to her group
    in class projects,
misses nonverbals,
ignores subtle aspersions,
rails against those who think she's
a robot—
emotionless.

An underachiever
    in her group
    asks her about
fun, if she can
relax,
    and she says
she'd like to.
    We may need to deal with
    family sacred cows.

High Achiever

This poem portrays a dramatic moment in a discussion in one of seven small groups that I facilitated at a middle school. I was attempting to see if the topic-oriented discussion format that I had used with gifted high school students would work as well with a younger age group. It did.

This group of seven—both boys and girls—included mostly high achievers, all of them serious. We met several times before they stopped framing the discussion with references to grade point averages and early SAT scores. These students weren't necessarily competitive with each other, but they were quite concerned about keeping up their straight-A averages.

When they finally relaxed, let their tense shoulders sag a little, and tuned in to each other in new ways, they were able to respond warmly, offer support, and commiserate. As I had seen so often in the high school groups, they were surprised (and relieved) to learn that others also had "weird" concerns, had trouble going to sleep, worried about what others thought of them, and had anxiety about academic and other kinds of performance.

On that day, the subject of this poem was as she had been for several weeks—needing to lead, tallying her achievements, needing to stay in control, needing to impress. She talked rapidly, eyes darting around the group. This time, a boy in the group sincerely asked her about relaxing. It was as if he had stepped on the brakes.

The Recommendation

"What can I write for him?"
he asked as we left on a Friday.
This teacher has a reputation:
the well-endowed
who don't perform
are damned for life.

I asked him if he'd seen
this brilliant one
named Incomplete
do the violin
Tuesday
at the concert.
No.
I mentioned that it's said
he practiced day and night.
It showed.

I remember when he showed us
in his lunch group
his 8 starts on an AP paper
(all astounding)
with perfectionism
leaving them unfinished.

When I wrote for him,
I told about
his music,
brilliance,
wit,
and character, too—
besides the grades.
I wouldn't want
to close the door,
assign the future,
by speaking only of this quarter
or this year
or stage.

The Recommendation

Too often, teachers, coaches, administrators, gifted education teachers and coordinators, and even parents do indeed "assign the future" to children based on performance or non-performance during the school years. I recall conversations in teachers' workrooms about students, regardless of school level, that reflected assumptions that underachievers would have a bleak future or that achievers would continue to be stellar performers. I was intrigued with these predictions. I had seen discrepant school-versus-future performance in immediate and extended family members, high school and college classmates, spouse and children, and students I taught. My awareness of these differences led me to an interest in adolescent development and, later, to a career change.

Adolescence is a time of tremendous social and emotional complexity. I learned, as a teacher, that students with high capability are highly idiosyncratic. However, I also recognized that they often have high levels of sensitivity to environmental stimuli, a phenomenon I later would learn more about at conferences and conventions related to educating gifted youth. Becoming acquainted with the concept of overexcitabilities through Michael Piechowski helped me to make sense of what I had observed in many gifted individuals.

The young man in this poem epitomized complexity, sensitivity, overexcitabilities, and intensities. I suspect that he had problems with sensory integration—perhaps feeling flooded with stimuli at every turn. I was in contact with him for a few years after graduation. He had a rough time adjusting to college in a distant city—residence hall life, professors he couldn't connect with, a perpetual idealism-vs.-realism conflict, and lingering feelings of loss from earlier life experiences. He returned home and eventually finished college there. By his mid-thirties, he had found a reasonably good fit in an unusual career.

Spoiled

I wonder what it's like for you
to worry about
       what the police know about him,
       what they will do with him,
       where he is now,
       whether paranoia and schizophrenia
            are hereditary,
       what the teachers know,
       what the effects will be
            of never having known a sane father,
       how to deal with shame,
       what he'll do if he discovers
            where you'll go to college,
       whether sinus headaches
            ever go away with age,
       what you'll do
            if you ever take the lid off.

I wonder what you'd say
to know that teachers
think you're spoiled.

Spoiled

What we see is not much of what is actually in front of us. My own research and discussion group work have helped me understand that some gifted kids have a lot to protect—and conceal. Significant adults focus on their talents, intelligence, and achievement. Showing vulnerability may not feel comfortable. High intelligence may in fact help gifted individuals hide distress.

The beautiful girl who inspired this poem was musically talented, bright, and intuitive. She had unusual composure and elegance and was probably envied by her female classmates. She wasn't an eager contributor in her discussion group, but she was among friends there, and I could see how much they appreciated her. Her wit was quick and dry, and I was glad she came regularly.

One day, to my surprise, she appeared at my office door in obvious distress. She asked if homebound instruction were a possibility for her. She explained that she simply could not be in school. Her eyes reflected her state, and I did not doubt her need, even though she didn't give me much information and I didn't ask for it. I promised I'd check out some options, and subsequently she did indeed have three weeks at home. I became a courier of assignments and someone to talk with—besides her concerned mother.

Formerly, her life had probably been fairly upper-middle class, but in recent years, it had become complicated in the areas reflected in the poem. One female teacher I initially approached about assignments prodded me to reveal details. She liked to be "in the know" and had mentioned in an earlier conversation that she knew the girl's family. I said I didn't know much about the situation, just that I believed it was important that the girl have time away from school stressors. I also said that, regardless, it wouldn't be appropriate for me to share details. At that point, the teacher said something like, "You don't get it. She's just spoiled!"

I was glad the discussion group had helped this girl trust me to be her advocate. Maybe the group experience helped her develop an expressive vocabulary—important in a high-stress time during adolescence. At the end of her first college year at a large university, I had a brief chat with her. Reminding me of her reticence in the discussion group, and possibly also reflecting a sensitivity to teachers' potential voyeurism, she commented that she appreciated *not* being known by her professors. Her comments made sense. Four years after she graduated, I heard that she was doing well, applying her pertinent degrees in foreign service.

Cause and Effect

Cause-and-effect Nicole,
too aware of expectations,
consequences,
and failure
(life like math,
with huge equal signs),
with her 3.9
and music excellence
in a rigid perfectionism,
unable to savor any good moment,
unforgiving of adults who disappoint,
unable to exchange supper duties
for three looming tests,
trying for eighteen years
to merit a hug,
feeling only guilty
about what college will cost
(especially when there are no guarantees).

"Would it have made a difference
if I had turned out different?"
she asked them.

"Maybe"
was the answer.

I tried unsuccessfully
to explain unconditional love.

Cause and Effect

During my years in various high schools, this student was one of my most memorable. She would frequently appear at my door late in the day, during the last part of her practice time in the music department, and we would have difficulty talking. I didn't yet have some important counseling skills. (I would have them later.) I wasn't sure what she wanted or needed, and she wasn't able to express her concerns, but we did have conversations. Eventually, I set a type of boundary. I invited her to stop in on Fridays, at the end of her practice period, to check in with me. We did that for more than two years. She was a complex, intriguing, sad, and questioning young woman, wondering about aspects of life that most her age probably were not concerned about.

This poem does not need much elaboration. However, what I learned from this student was that it is important—sometimes for their very survival—for gifted students to have such conversations, even though those exchanges may not seem productive at the time. Several years later, I learned that this young woman had made serious attempts at suicide during college, eventually dropping out for a few years and receiving help before finishing her degree closer to home. She contacted me after graduation and told me that having those weekly conversations during high school were crucial to her survival then. She wanted me to know.

I have since studied resilience. One factor of resilience, according to various scholars, is having a mentor, a supporter, a surrogate parent, a "believer." When we are available, credible, and genuine, and when we give students reason to trust us, resist judgment, and allow them to "just be," we may become that crucial factor. It was important that I was *there*. It was important that I met her *where she was* at that time in her life.

A Memorable Experience

Your application essay
for college
told them how you did it,
washing the pills down
with Evian water,
pure,
like Communion.
It described emergency-room humor,
the first therapy (mediocre),
family therapy (good),
relief,
and what you learned
for life
at seventeen.

A Memorable Experience

This troubled adolescent joined a discussion group at the beginning of her sophomore year. Her sister, a high achiever, was in another group—presenting herself much differently from this seemingly rebellious young woman. One difference was this one's strong interest in the visual arts. She also joined a weekly early morning poetry club, during which she and other underachievers played with language and wrote brief poems in response to serious and silly prompts and also shared what they had written during the week. They took turns bringing juice and muffins or donuts. This attractive, articulate, sensitive, and passionate girl expressed herself nimbly on paper, but I sensed that her learning style was not a good fit with traditional teaching styles. She said she was more comfortable in a small group than in a full classroom.

She attended the noon-hour discussion group and morning poetry meetings faithfully. Then, late in her junior year, she was absent for a while. When she returned the next year, we became aware that she had made a serious suicide attempt, which led to an unraveling of intra-family complexities. Her father's death a few years earlier had precipitated distressing family patterns that had endured. In therapy, according to an extended metaphor in her application essay, puzzle pieces were taken apart, examined, and reassembled positively.

She was not the first gifted senior who asked my opinion about writing an essay based on a tragedy. But it was indeed the first time someone thought she should write about her suicide attempt. It had been a life-changing event, and it was all she could think of when one university asked for a memorable experience. She wrote the essay and let me read it. It was eloquent and powerful. As I recall, she was accepted there but decided to go somewhere else.

I heard later that her college years were good ones. She was certainly not the only adolescent whose poor academic performance reflected emotional distress and family tension during high school. She was fortunate that her mother and step-father invested in healing—thoroughly and at many levels. She was also fortunate that they recognized and affirmed her uniqueness and her intelligence, even during her underachieving years. The poetry club was one of several program components that took the pressure off, encouraged reflection and expression, and offered crucial support during her and others' difficult adolescence.

The Writing on the Wall

His essay was smooth and clear,
unfancy,
in male style,
posted on the wall for conferences
as a model of quality.
There was interpretation
and analysis,
not summary.
It was incisive and lean.
He had caught the themes.

I couldn't understand
his burly trucker father,
who winced when I said
he must be proud
of the fine mind
he had begotten
and the fine product on the wall.
Those tenured in town
told me later
I should have understood.

This blond Adonis,
with words only on paper
and enigmatic eyes,
a quiet coordination in football,
the little boy still played with trucks
to be with Dad.

The ivory tower
separated him further
than his good writing had,
and he dropped and drifted
with alcohol.
A romantic rejection,
and he shot himself.

I think about
the writing on the wall.

The Writing on the Wall

This sad poem reminds me not only of this handsome, pensive young athlete who almost never spoke in English class, but also of the power and impact of developing complex writing skills. My students never wrote "personal journals," since I consider those to be voyeuristic. But they were encouraged to respond on paper each week to the literature they read. We studied vocabulary from the novels ahead of each unit, and during the unit, I provided background by bringing in speakers, lecturing on a pertinent historical period or figure, or even showing a travel video. Eventually, the students gathered their thoughts into coherent papers. There was no "correct" interpretation. There were no quizzes or exams. They simply wrote about the themes that had emerged in their readings and in their journals. I hardly ever lectured on the novels themselves.

Later, I would learn that mutual learning (students and teacher), tolerance for ambiguity and "not knowing," dialectical discourse, personalized learning, and experiential learning all characterize this approach. Most important, this approach to studying literature is open-ended. Gifted students can dig in as deeply as they want to. Low-average students can do the same. They can write about what they think is important—often about complex characters. I evaluated their writing, making sure that they received credible, constructive feedback, and I was moved by their progress.

This young man was one of my best students the year that he took my sophomore Novels class. I've often wondered if he was struggling emotionally then, if he had difficulty connecting to his father then or only later, and if having opportunities to talk about social and emotional development as an adolescent would have helped him survive heartbreak as a young adult. Other students sometimes wrote about difficult personal situations that were related to what they were reading, but I saw no evidence of distress in his Novels journal. Was it just in English class that he was silent? Did the macho environment of athletics inhibit expression? Did anyone in college or in the family know that he was so vulnerable? When I became a counselor focusing on gifted kids and their families, I became convinced that a venue for oral expression related to growing up and developing socially and emotionally is both urgent and crucial in gifted programs—and unfortunately almost always absent. Even a small amount of training for gifted education personnel can go a long way toward helping them connect to gifted students comfortably, appropriately, and non-voyeuristically. Skills related to effective expression of feelings may be especially important when the road is rough.

In the Resistance

Her parents worry
over grades and
her dropout boyfriend
and want a recipe
for a quick fix.

I talk about self-esteem
and definitions based on low grades
and her good discussion group,
where she is wise and articulate
and hungry for affirmation
and smart enough
to resist all parental tricks.

In the Resistance

Before I met this underachieving sophomore, her high-achieving, prodigiously talented sister had, just prior to graduation, asked me to "look out for my little sister." The older sibling said her sister was smart, but the younger sister did not believe that. Later, during group interaction, I concluded that the older sister's observation was accurate.

These groups purposefully included both high academic performers and low performers. I believed then, as I do now, that underachievement in gifted kids is largely developmental, and I wanted some non-academic program components that would embrace and accommodate those who either couldn't or wouldn't (at that time in their lives) focus on academics. These activities brought them into contact with others with high ability who could affirm and support them during adolescence. I usually went around the table at the first group meeting, asking each student to tell the group where they "let their intelligence show." I made it clear that the data in their school file showed that they indeed had high capability, but I was curious about how it was demonstrated. This young woman immediately claimed that she "wasn't intelligent," not unlike how underachievers often responded. After a little prodding, she admitted that she was "pretty good" in art and wrote some music for a band she was in. That was helpful information for me and for other group members, since, in that large high school, students often were not acquainted with each other. From that day on, she invested in her delightful group. Some—also underachievers—were her friends. At first, the high achievers were surprised to see the underachievers in the group, but they quickly relaxed and learned from them. As often was the case in the groups, the underachievers were more expressive about social and emotional development. I wondered if that reflected that they'd had to define themselves against others' expectations.

Later, I asked this young woman if I could study her (among several in her graduating class) over the next four years, staying in touch through letters and questionnaires related to developmental tasks. She and several others agreed, and I was able to participate, from afar, in their development of identity, autonomy, career direction, movement toward a mature relationship, and differentiation in the form of resolution of conflict with family. After four years, she had moved ahead in all of these areas but was still struggling with low self-esteem and had not securely accomplished any of the tasks. Her parents, though certainly not wealthy, had funded some unusual experiences as she found her way, including ecology-oriented service-learning projects in the United States and abroad. At the end of the study, she planned to register at a small, reputable college that I expected would fit her altruism. She wrote that she felt apprehensive but knew it was time to invest. My last contact with her was when she invited me to donate to a bike-riding event that would cross the country during the summer for a cause.

From A to Z

His pale, motionless intensity,
when I tell him about himself,
belies his flippant, boyish cool.
He schemes and dreams. Money means
success, and it is effortless and lazy,
getting it and keeping it, he says.
We talk of getting from A to Z
in small steps. I chill, watching
his languid, handsome roll exit
the office and move to study hall
to ponder direct routes to Z.

From A to Z

This was a long, unforgettable moment with a significantly under-achieving junior. I don't know what had contributed to his lack of investment and low performance in academic work. His parents were divorced. He was the younger of two children, the older an achieving sister. These might have been factors, of course, but I view underachievement as too complex for easy cause-effect thinking about it.

Test scores revealed that he had high ability. However, he did not sign up for any program options, and he declined my invitation to join a group. I talked with him on this occasion because one of his parents had requested it. We talked about his interest in business, but his view of the future was vague. He had said that his affluent relatives really didn't "do anything" but neverthe-less did well financially. He did not connect current academic work to future employment, nor effort with achievement. I knew I would probably not have a chance to talk with him again, and I felt both frustrated and sad as he left.

This young man epitomizes what I began to think of as a "limp" kind of academic underachievement. Perhaps it is a passive-aggressive way to deal with loss and expectations—choosing not to perform. Perhaps it is developmental stuckness, reflecting an inability to focus and move ahead in one or more areas.

The conversation that prompted this poem left me feeling that this teen's vision of the future was a vanishing line that did not include steps and stages, but I also wondered if depression and anxiety were involved. I was not a coun-selor at that point and did not have the skills I needed to engage him.

Eating Disorder

She sees me leaving
after her three quiet years
in my groups
and knows she must say it now
or maybe wait forever,
so she writes the note,
knowing I will send one, too,
reads the pages that I copy,
takes the videotape home to watch
while her mom is at work
and puts "Thanks" with it on my desk
Monday morning.

Eating Disorder

In late May, this young woman, ready to graduate, stopped in after school and began, "Remember when we talked about eating disorders in group? Well, I've had one for a long time, and I know I need to deal with this before I leave for college."

I had made and long kept a videotape of a lecture on the topic. The speaker had been part of an after-school gifted education series titled "Living in the Age of Anxiety," presented by medical professionals and open to anyone in school. It was an especially effective presentation, but this was my first opportunity to loan the videotape. Before she left with it, she said, "I've done everything my parents and coaches have asked me to do—expected me to do. Straight A's, success in extracurriculars, well-behaved. But I don't know who I am."

Her words stayed with me. I think of them sometimes when I interact with tense, perfectionistic high achievers who seem constrained and vaguely uncertain. I sense that control is preferable to the risks of venturing into uncharted territory. In contrast, I have sometimes wondered if some students who are able to perform academically but who willfully choose not to may move more effectively along a continuum of identity development by trying on different personas, resisting parental or teacher expectations, causing commotion with invested adults, and behaving *against* expectations. Some underachievers seem paralyzed, unable to move ahead. But those who actively challenge, resist, rebel, or simply discover and follow their bliss at an early age seem more free to explore the self. This senior, who probably represented an ideal for most adults, was concerned that she had not done this. She connected it to the eating disorder.

She participated in a follow-up study of her gifted classmates four years after they graduated. She wrote, in an accompanying note, that someone close to her had died during college, but she had dealt with that—over time—without reverting to disordered eating. I trust that she continued to do well.

Victim

A victim
of the proverbial uncle
suffering now
with an abusive boyfriend
who chips at her
this pretty intellect
of low self-esteem
from the wrong side
with a 4.0 as balance
even with black eyes
from no sleep
and him
even with absences
that rankle teachers
she knows now
she is only the most recent
in a long family history
with the vault door tight
needs more than cheap therapy
makes a second attempt
at ending things
we are relieved to hear
she will finish the year
in an alternative place
that needs to be bigger.

Victim

Gifted children and adolescents are not exempt from sexual abuse, domestic violence, severe family dysfunction, trauma, and other tragic life situations. Parents may fight, separate, and divorce; families may blend, and children may lose their place in the new arrangement. Families may relocate again and again, disrupting peer relationships. Parents may become unemployed, be incarcerated, be deployed for military duty, be addicted to dangerous substances, or be absent. Family members or the children themselves may become seriously ill, injured, or disabled. They may experience loss in other ways as well, such as loss of "the way it used to be," loss of friendships, loss of a safe and secure environment, or loss of innocence.

With their sensitivities and intensities, trauma and loss may be even more difficult for gifted children to overcome than for others their age. They may apply their intellectual strengths in trying to make sense of their situations, but their social and emotional development is likely not comparably advanced, and they may despair. At a young age, their probable lack of life experience may make it difficult to put situations into perspective. On the other hand, intelligence is a factor of resilience, and cognitive strengths can help them problem solve, plan realistically for the future, and find resources to help them heal.

I include this poem here as an example of trauma and many kinds of losses. When this brave girl came with her mother to tell me about her suicide attempt and what had come to light in the aftermath as the women in her extended family told their stories, there was relief in their faces. The shared experience had been named. Something would be done. They would go for help, although I had some doubts about who they preferred for that help. There was a lot to repair, and the process would likely last a long time.

The Writer

When he froze his ears
after his car stalled
and he ran home
in a hefty wind chill,
we noticed him collectively
for days,
discussed in the lounge the ears
of this one
with pitted face
(as I recall),
blank affect,
no voice to recall
even when they took turns in answers.
But his writing
(in an awkward hand
on an awkward body)
arrested me
(I can still envision it),
his poetic prose
plumbing the complexities
of what we read.
It made me raise my eyes
and look for long moments
into the distance.
I know my friend recruited him
the next year
for the paper,
but then I moved.
I wonder where
he ended up.

The Writer

I wrote this poem because I wanted to be reminded, in my work as an educator, that kids we call "gifted" frequently do not fit common stereotypes and often fly under the radar. We should be cautious about generalizing with statements beginning "Gifted kids are…." There are few characteristics that apply to all, and even these vary in degree. Cultures and contexts also vary—even about what kinds of strengths and talents are deemed "gifted." Research samples representing giftedness also vary, with contexts and criteria for identification potentially skewing the results. In addition, there are great ability differences among gifted children. The upper end of the bell curve of intellectual ability, representing giftedness, can be extremely long in terms of range of scores on assessments.

English teachers who take writing development seriously and invest in it have a rare window into their students' inner world. It was my students' writing in response to literature that gave me a unique vantage point—and an eventual research direction. Quiet, intense, highly observant students like the subject of this poem gave me some of the most memorable surprises.

His sophomore English class was rather large. He communicated on paper, and I responded with notes in the margins. I read his papers eagerly, and I regret that I didn't find a way to talk with him and learn more about his life—beyond his experience in the bitter cold, which did generate a short conversation before class began that day. If a program had existed, and if he had chosen to participate in it, a discussion group for gifted kids might have been a boon for him during those years.

This young man was white, rural, probably lower-middle class economically, uninvolved in extracurricular activities, an introvert, not social, and unassertive. There was no special program for gifted kids in that high school, and I wonder if he would have been identified even if one had existed, given his quiet, non-interactive personality. If not given somewhat open-ended writing assignments about complex literature, would his bright mind have had a chance to express itself? How would his wonderful vocabulary be observed so that a teacher could check that item on a referral form for a program? How would he demonstrate insight, unusual ideas, a keen sense of humor, intense concern about social justice and moral issues, intellectual playfulness, or advanced interpretations (also frequently on the checklists) if he never spoke in the classroom?

The Parent

This one
12
identified gifted
abused by the two younger
for being bossy
worries
that video games
will make Brother
like Father
prods Mom
to get to work on time
frets about what Brother packs
for lunch.

This same one
is the parent
sobs
maybe for the first time
exhausted
doesn't know
how long he can hold on
knows she probably can't change
is the one
in fragile control
could be 40
sitting tensely
under thin shoulders
waiting to disintegrate.

The Parent

When preparing graduate students to be counselors, I use this situation to illustrate the concept of *parentification*, a phenomenon in which children assume inappropriate adult roles in their families. The expected family leadership hierarchy is "upset," since the child, not the parent, is the family leader. This may occur when parents are physically or emotionally absent, addicted, seriously ill, experiencing long-term depression, or in childlike roles. A parent who treats a child or adolescent as an adult confidante or peer also gives the young family member inappropriate responsibility. Children at many levels of intelligence assume parental roles out of necessity, of course. However, gifted children may be especially likely to step into such roles, with their able minds, talents, skills, and common sense. Even in only moderately problematic circumstances, gifted children may be deferred to inappropriately for major family decisions, for instance. Their parents may not be aware that they are treating the children as adults in more ways than just with adult conversation.

This phenomenon is worrisome because these children may become the "bottom line" in the family—the individual who must call tough shots in crises to keep the family functioning. In a family with an alcoholic adult, children without enough life experience or wisdom to recognize potential ramifications may beg the non-alcoholic parent to stay. When both parents are incapacitated, even a young child may manage the home. When a home is unsafe, a child or teen may assume the role of protector of siblings. Emotionally, it can be frightening to a young child or teen—or even an older teen—not to have responsible adults to rely on for protection, decisions, and nurturance. Developmentally, the child is robbed of a normal childhood. Regardless of how cognitively advanced a child or teen is, being parentified usually involves anxiety, pressure, fear of tomorrow, and fear for the future. It may be difficult for them to imagine a time without such responsibilities.

The boy in this portrait is easy for me to bring to mind. He is sitting in front of me during a family counseling session, frightened and frantically saying, "I don't think I can hold on." His mother sits to one side with a puzzled, childlike expression, and his two younger siblings sit soberly on the other side. Grandma has managed the home, but she is now impaired and elderly. Mom has never had those responsibilities. This gifted boy has assumed the roles, but they are too heavy and not appropriate for his age.

Three Boys

"When do you feel out of control?"
I asked their group.

Brad said
his violin mentor
put on Brahms's Fourth
and then smiled
as Brad felt
out of control.

Chad said
he felt out of control
angry.

Thad had worried over
his rage
on Sunday
when the friend
who lives with them now
invaded
a precious time
with his two-month
(a new record)
girlfriend.

Three Boys

This poem represents how engaging (and needed) focused discussion about growing up can be for gifted kids. The focus for group discussion that week was "In Control, Out of Control." I had wondered whether the topic would generate discussion, but I wanted to tap into the sensitivities and intensities that I had been seeing in gifted students. I thought that approaching the process of growing up through a discussion of control had potential.

It was an unforgettable discussion—for me, certainly, but perhaps also for them. They first talked about when they felt comfortable and in control. They mentioned specific classes and academic domains, talent expression, athletics, being with friends, reading, and lying in bed after waking up. Their antennae bristled with expectation and excitement when they connected with each other about some area.

Then the discussion became intense and even more serious as they considered where and when they felt out of control. Their eyes narrowed or widened, depending on what they were describing—and they did indeed describe some situations in detail. Eyes flashed with recognition and resonance when something unexpected or particularly interesting was mentioned by someone in the group. They talked about hormones; conflicts with parents; being bullied by peers, siblings, and even teachers; being in love; unrequited love; being fired from a job; feeling sad; experiencing the death of someone close; perfectionism; procrastination; crying at a funeral; feeling rage.

What they were learning was how to reflect on and express feelings. They were developing an expressive vocabulary, which, as I sometimes said to them, might help them sustain an important relationship someday, as well as employment, and might help them be solid, approachable, appreciated parents. But just as important was their connecting with each other that day, in the present, and finding common ground at a developmentally challenging time.

Goosebumps

He got an A in AP History
and a B in physics,
and I got goosebumps
when his dad showed me
at conferences.

It had been a long time.

But his poetry showed the spark,
and I remember he lately said
(about college),
"I think I'm ready to be a student now."

Goosebumps

This young man had an extremely high IQ but was achieving academically far below expectations until his senior year. Only then did he gradually become more approachable, more engaged with peers, more communicative, more personable. We all enjoyed him in his lunch-hour discussion group and at before-school poetry meetings. He was actually a leader in the latter. His divorced father, with whom he had lived for many years, had been patient, and his happy eyes teared up when he showed me the report card. Development? Yes, indeed. Sometimes accomplishing key developmental tasks leads to motivation to achieve academically.

If underachievement is sometimes simply (and complexly) developmental, then adults can communicate hope to low performers that multi-level change is not only possible, but inevitable. Nothing, bad or good, stays exactly the same. Situations change, people change, and kids grow up. Perhaps the change is finally being able to focus and concentrate in school and in life, to feel a sense of career direction, to have fewer distractions, to resolve conflict with family, to gain autonomy, to have a mature relationship with a special person. Maybe two or even more of these developmental challenges will be resolved at about the same time. Life might jerk forward almost suddenly— no longer "stuck." If academic achievement is valued and desirable, there might then be motivation to move in that direction.

A low-motivation gifted junior reported in his group that his mother had said, a few times in recent years, that she trusted that he'd "figure it out" himself sometime—although she didn't know if it would be next week or 10 years down the road. Four years after high school, he had a degree in an area of science, after comfortable "B" work throughout college, and was a happy, satisfied young man at a very good place in life. He continued in that mode into adulthood and a profession. I have since used his mother's comment with underachieving kids and their parents myself, grateful that her son shared it with us.

Warm Eyes

Teary, warm eyes and a quivering lip with his
head angled down in our long conversation,
distressed over what someone said two years prior,
too tall for his age, he assumes expectation for
sports (and he's clumsy, of course). He speaks sadly
of father, his hero, who's witty, too busy,
forgiven when not there enough, but prescribing
protection to ward off the demons he lived with
himself as a lonely, deficient-attention kid,
just like this son, who, with Ritalin, Prozac,
Imipramine, tracks better now, gets good grades,
but feels arrows in glances, would die to be popular,
chokes when he talks to a female, feels focus from
all in a group, sorely vulnerable, wounded,
grave doubts when he's told it gets better with age.
We will work on the social this year, and I'll call
if I doubt all the chemicals. Group members can,
if I do it well, give him the feedback he needs,
so that angry, sad features can smile.

Warm Eyes

I clearly recall this handsome, earnest eighth grader and his noon-hour discussion group on that day, even though many years have passed since they spent a semester around a table in a small conference room. I sat quietly after the group left, still moved by how much his comments had resonated with the rest of them. They seemed to connect with him and with each other when he spoke of his problems with attention, self-consciousness, awkwardness, angst, fears about the future, and awareness of peers who seemed "to have it all together." He was 14, and these feelings and experiences are not unusual during early adolescence. In the safety of the group, which by then had established a good level of trust, they leaned in, spoke soberly, gave eye contact comfortably, and put their vague sadness on the table.

It's difficult to know exactly how different the subjective experience with normal developmental tasks is for gifted children and adolescents in comparison with others their age. Scholars have only rarely explored this area. Quantitative methods are unlikely to ferret out such distinctions. Sensitive responses require trust in peers, and gifted teens are often protective of the image of success that they have honed—or, in contrast, an image of non-performance. What they probably do not know is that their sensitivities, anxieties, feelings, concerns, and desires are not uncommon—among gifted kids and probably among others as well. Scholars who focus on giftedness have argued that the difference for gifted youth is a matter of degree.

To Hear Better

I was no different—
took his averted eyes
as insult,
boredom,
and felt like shaking his lapels,
angry
at the seeming arrogance,
a tuning out
by turning down
when others spoke.

I called him in
to talk about the effect
on the group
(I should have said "on me").
He said
he couldn't concentrate—
an overstimulation
when he looked
at the speaker—
couldn't hear
unless he looked down.

To Hear Better

It was an instructive moment for me. I often refer to it when speaking to groups about characteristics associated with giftedness in the clinical and research literature. Invariably, some heads nod, with sober facial expressions. Psychoeducational information like this can help students, parents, teachers, and peers make sense of feelings and behaviors in self and others that seem odd. Like me at that time, teachers and parents and other significant adults may not be aware of this phenomenon and may be judgmental. I obviously misread this boy's behavior. I'm glad he could explain it to me. Perhaps other gifted children with this kind of sensitivity are not as self-aware or as articulate as he was. Learning about sensory overexcitability might help them make sense of themselves.

In his discussion group, this sophomore was quiet and seemed vaguely sad. He usually spoke only when group members were asked to read what they had written on an "activity sheet." There was no cockiness, but he had great presence in his group, and I sensed that others were concerned that he'd think their comments were "dumb." They often checked him out after I posed a question, even though he rarely gave eye contact. Maybe they were in awe of his legendary intellect. Maybe it was because he said so little. Maybe it was his somber aura. Regardless, I blamed him for the group's lack of spontaneity.

What he taught me that day in my office was about sensitivity to incoming environmental stimulation, all of it being enormously distracting for him. Adding visual stimulation to the auditory, tactile, and ambient would have interfered with his being able to focus on what was said. So he was actually being respectful of others as he also struggled to handle what his brain was processing. Since then, I have known others who have described a complex, debilitating "overload" of stimulation. The subject of this poem began my education about this kind of sensitivity.

In college, campus life was generally not comfortable for him. However, he eventually applied his extensive experience in music to his own small business: stringed instrument construction and repair. That work context probably was a good fit for his sensitivities.

Eighth Grader

Because one hundred
are absent with flu,
only three girls come to group,
and she says
she feels safe
in the exercise about
PERMISSION
to say that she needs it
to BE INTELLIGENT,
among several things,
because the risk
is great
in eighth grade,
guys don't like big words
in girls,
she says,
and counselors play it safe
for career suggestions,
and a military father
abides no disagreement
about politics
or house rules,
and being liked
and nice
is most important,
so she's thought it best
to stuff "intelligent"
for now.

Eighth Grader

This girl took advantage of the forthright, respectful group to explore her concern about whether demonstrating a high level of intelligence and having a social life could coexist. Her group normally included both genders, and it was interesting that she saw the all-girl group that day as a chance to explore this topic. She had been quiet until now, and this was a change. She talked at length, elaborating on areas named in the poem.

Scholars, clinicians, convention presenters, teachers, program coordinators, and parents often mention this social dilemma when sharing thoughts about gifted students' developmental struggles. It is reflected in girls' opting out of advanced math and other challenging courses during middle and high school. Adults then worry that career gates will close for them—maybe forever.

Boys may also choose not to show their ability. Reasons behind either gender's hiding high ability may indeed be related to social needs and fears. However, the hiding may, for some individuals, also reflect feelings about adult models who represent difficulties with, or negative biases about, high ability and how it is demonstrated and applied.

Developmental challenges also drive the hiding phenomenon. Gifted students, like others their age, are probably asking questions related to identity development ("Who am I?"), differentiation from family ("Who am I, separate from and yet connected to my parents and siblings?" "Why do I fight with my parents?"), direction ("What should I do with my life?"), relationships ("Will I have friends, be married someday, be around people I like?"), and autonomy ("I don't want people telling me what to do. How can I be independent?").

Gifted teens, like anyone else, want to make sense of their struggles. They apply their exceptional cognitive abilities, but those abilities are often not enough for sense-making. When interacting with them, especially after the teens have been able to express social concerns, adults can frame social difficulties as "making sense" developmentally. Feelings and behaviors usually do make sense in the context of identity and relational development. Making sense doesn't mean that these problems immediately disappear, of course, but "normalizing" social concerns may actually tone them down enough to be put into perspective.

In that eighth-grade group, the three girls thoughtfully discussed being intellectually gifted. I didn't need to say much at all. At the end, they said that they had never talked about this topic "out loud" and with such intense focus. I was inspired by how they had addressed the topic so insightfully and eagerly. My sense was that they found courage and clarity through doing it.

He Has Edges

not yet
can he say
he practices
violin
or studies
for tests
not yet
can he cry
his agony
not yet
be soft
can
be only
angry
about the father
the uncle
the grandpa
the life
two deaths
in those men
so far
three
in peers
this year
heart attacks
in the father

he has a short fuse
and rage
that goes 95
on country roads
because
that's
what men do
on his side
of town.

He Has Edges

Based on appearance, dress, and manner, he did not look like a musician. He didn't fit that stereotype. But he and his orchestra peers were comfortable with each other in his discussion group, and their sharp and subtle humor and chuckling often rippled suddenly from shore to shore during discussions. He claimed he never studied but got A's. When his fellow musicians joked or complained about something related to orchestra, he studiously made the point that he took music lightly. However, when I once casually, just out of curiosity, asked the conductor about how the musicians in the gifted program were to work with, he said that this guy was good—and serious.

The discussion that inspired this poem occurred a week or so after a tragic accident had killed a junior on a motorcycle in the parking lot. The victim was his friend. Without stopping, after referring to the accident, he proceeded to talk about the deaths in his extended family and his fears for his father—as soberly as he had ever spoken to us. We sat silently, absorbed in his sadness and concerns, trying to imagine ourselves in his tense and watchful world. I asked how he was coping—how he was managing his life and his emotions. That's when he told us how he drove, drove, drove—very fast—until he felt solid enough to go home and sleep.

I never met his parents and knew very little about his home situation. As far as I know, he had no siblings in the school. He joined a Future Problem Solving team one year and was appreciated for what he offered. I wish he had joined the breakfast poetry meetings. Maybe I would have sensed more paradoxes.

Hunk

he is beautiful
and controlled
even his walk
has no ripples
lived with his mom
an only child
after the divorce
got into the wrong crowd
moved in with his dad
at seventeen
after too many arguments
he's out
living with a friend
too possessive of his girl
who won't give him exclusivity
today he felt like crying
in an out-of-control
different from rage
I told him I was glad
he didn't leave

with tears
and a sheepish smile
he said
he missed his mom

Hunk

The poem needs little elaboration regarding that part of his story. However, this boy's role in his discussion group, two additional program components geared to supporting students like him, and his post-secondary development are all pertinent here and worth discussing. He was a natural, effortless leader, with considerable presence in his group. Because he was genuine, self-effacing, serious, and forthcoming about his troubles, they "became a group" much more quickly than others that year. If he had been quiet, or sullen, or withdrawn, probably no other group members would have spoken. They would have wondered whether he would approve or be critical of their comments. Model-handsome males often have that kind of power. So do beautiful females. But he was not into power, and his receptive, cooperative, and expressive mode was contagious.

As part of an after-school lecture series, I brought in a former state governor who lived nearby. He'd had a troubled childhood and had tangled with the courts as a juvenile. Those stories became media fodder now and then. He explained to his audience that he took dangerous risks and fought with his step-father, who, he realized later, was a wonderful man he could have learned from. This former governor spoke of a learning disability, as well as being a rebel even in college. He was also willing, when I asked, to meet with a group of boys who were similarly square pegs in round holes. "Hunk" came to my office after the latter presentation, clearly moved by what he had just experienced. He said, "I had no idea he was like me."

I later met a member of the Chamber of Commerce during a Kiwanis Club meeting where I had spoken about "at-risk gifted kids." I had said that I wished those kids could meet successful adults who had needed support and guidance themselves as adolescents. This gentleman volunteered, and I arranged for him to meet with the boy whose early life story is in the poem. Again, a successful man who had struggled as an adolescent generated hope.

I followed this young man's career for four years after he graduated. He briefly attended college but realized it wasn't what he wanted at that time. By the second or third year, he figured out that he needed to take the initiative in building a relationship with his father and step-mother, and he did that. By the fourth year, he had become a Ford model, with some international travel in connection with his work. He said he had grown up, had learned from complicated relationships, and was doing "well enough."

Common Denominators

My Friday group
found common denominators:
headaches, insomnia, anxiety,
and future-fear.
Each had a special range
of stress symptoms,
and each had a coping strategy:
sleep, exercise, music,
withdrawal,
conversation.
Jake was again the star
when he said he cried.

Common Denominators

In facilitating development-oriented discussion groups, whether with high school, middle school, or elementary-age gifted children, I make sure that stress is the focus of at least one session. During students' first year in the high school groups, there are usually three meetings during which these questions are addressed: (1) What is stress, and how is it manifested? (2) How can stress be "dissected" so that it can be understood and feel less overwhelming? (3) What are some ineffective ways that adults and age peers cope with it? (4) What strategies seem to be effective? (5) What might be one coping strategy that you could add to your current arsenal?

According to group discussions, and according to a study mentioned in the Introduction to this volume, the heaviest stressors during the high school years are related to Advanced Placement courses, part-time jobs, heavy extracurricular activities, and service projects. In the study, although many students had experienced deaths in their extended family, serious illnesses, traumatic situations, relocations, and other major changes and losses, school was the stressor mentioned most often when these teens reviewed their school years just prior to graduation. School transitions and peer relationships were also often mentioned.

As my friend Sal Mendaglio has emphasized in his important work related to giftedness, rapid information processing means that gifted individuals may be hyper-responsive to sensory stimuli and consequently affected emotionally by that environmental information. Including details about stress in a gifted education curriculum can help gifted kids understand their sensitivities and intensities and cope with common and uncommon stressors. In my research of gifted underachievers, trauma survivors, targets of bullying, and children of substance abusers, I have found that highly able individuals try to make sense of difficulties on their own. In doing so, they may achieve a sense of at least *cognitive* control of their situations.

Jake was a valued, genuine, thought-provoking member of his group. When he said that he cried, everyone was at first startled—and then nodded in agreement. Then they all opened up about how stressed they were feeling with papers, projects, and tests looming.

Persistence

he never misses group
we greet him warmly
but he rarely speaks
this strange one
eyes down
doodling microscopically
we are a world
he does not know
his mentor dad
died
his mom
off balance
drew the tether tight
and short
he connects tenuously
to us
puts words
in the end
on his hair-trigger temper
on complex thoughts
begins the horn again
compulsively
earns their respect
fails all five classes
can't ask for help
the data
call him gifted
and we will persist

Persistence

I don't know what happened to this complex student, partly because I moved away at the end of that school year, and he eventually moved as well. I hope he managed the next several years well enough, and I hope he had a chance to work with a good counselor sometime—especially as he moved into adulthood and continued to sort himself out.

I was impressed by how the others in his group supported him. He gradually gained enough trust and composure to talk, using words sparingly, about how he and his military father had explored the Southwest, discussing scientific and other things. He appeared to still be in shock at the loss of his dad. He indicated that his life had unraveled, at the same time becoming tightly circumscribed. He talked about his temper—particularly how it came out at home—interspersing some details with a caustic chuckle that kept his peers silent and still. Little by little over the next weeks, he became more engaged in discussion, at least during the "go-arounds," when each student, in turn, shared a response to a sentence stem or an item that they had checked on a list. His relationship with the group was a taut thread, but it was indeed a developing relationship.

The others paid attention to him, involved him in small talk as they settled in for their hour-long meeting, commented about his investment in band, and provoked a tense smile in him now and then. It was a moving experience, and I was pleased to see the effects of the kindness and sensitivity of his gifted peers. It is possible that he might otherwise have had little or no conversation with anyone at school.

For this young man, picking up the horn again probably represented a big step out of despair and into something that reminded him of a happier time, although that process might also have been unsettling. Maybe his grades started improving, too, but maybe not. Most significant to his well-being, at that time, were social and emotional concerns. Pressing him about academic work might have stopped his movement forward altogether. My guess is that neither school nor schoolwork felt controllable during those turbulent years.

He Couldn't Wait

he had absorbed his mother's
fervor
for finding a third husband
one with money
this time
for college educations
and things
for all of them
when it seemed to work out
he studied qualities and names
of cameras and computers
clothes and cars
and colleges
but then it didn't work out
so we wrote letters
about his many gifts
and with his grades
he won a full ride
in pre-med
to an important place
such emotional confusion
when the lawyer called me in July
for a character deposition
after he was caught
dealing drugs
he couldn't wait

He Couldn't Wait

I had surmised early on that this teen was close to his mother and that there was mutual respect between them. Her solid support was apparent at parent-teacher conferences, and I assume he'd had the role of "man of the house" when she was between marriages. He was excited when prospects for her looked good, and it was clear that he and his younger siblings believed she had the kids in mind when she considered a new relationship for herself.

The experiences portrayed in this poem reflect themes that I saw in the lives of many students I taught: caring parents in challenging circumstances, kids responding to unpredictable life events, lack of financial security, precarious future plans, and preoccupation with gaining some control over a complex life. I trust that some of these students developed enough resilience to overcome adversities. Some, like this student, performed well academically—despite their difficulties and perhaps also because of them. For some gifted individuals, performing well not only provides some control, but also serves as insurance for the future.

I was sad that this boy had likely lost his laboriously created insurance plan, since he'd now have a felony on his record. However, his resilience, honed on lack of security, is probably what helped him find employment and make a life for himself. Two years later, as I lay on a cart in an elevator, groggy and on my way to surgery, I heard a voice say, "Hi, Mrs. Peterson." He was the orderly steering me in the right direction, happy to be working in a hospital and saying he had plans.

Poor Speller

With at least three words per line
in his strange script
misspelled,
I always left his until last.
They were hard to decipher,
and with 140 that year
I needed to get through 20
the first night
for momentum.
But what he wrote—
much better than his speech impediment
    could manage—
was among the most incisive
in those days before gifted programs.

I wonder if he asked
for special dispensation
in college.
I told him
to find a good speller
for a roommate.
Even Spell-check probably
would have been confused.

Poor Speller

This poem features a student I taught long before I became formally involved in the education of gifted students. He and others with intriguing personalities and exceptional ability grabbed my attention, and I would often have an emotional response to their insights and ability to articulate complex thoughts and phenomena on paper.

What made his papers stand out was not only the complexity of his thoughts and sentence structure, but also how he mangled the spelling of even relatively simple words. Usually those two extremes are not found in the same paper. He probably was the first student to impress on me that there could be dual exceptionality—that is, a significant learning disability *and* extremely high ability in at least one academic domain. The physics teacher told me that this boy had impressive ability in science. He wasn't a high-profile student. He wasn't involved in extracurricular activities, and he had a fairly nondescript presence in class. But he was alert, with his eyes on mine when I scanned the class or on others when they spoke.

Looking back, I recall other twice-exceptional students. One boy in my tenth-grade remedial English class had never read a complete book yet managed to wade through *Of Mice and Men*. It was typically the first paperback I put into the students' hands. The vocabulary was basic enough, action grabbed their attention from the outset, the theme of loneliness pervading the book resonated with them, and they appreciated that John Steinbeck was a famous writer and the book has been a movie. This boy told me that he'd always had a reading problem but had figured out that he could manage to read when he was very tired, late at night, when his brain would allow it. The book was thoroughly dog-eared when he finished, but he was eager to start another.

Later in my career, an eleventh grader was recommended for a gifted program by a drafting teacher who wanted me to "check him out." He had been receiving special education support for many years for a significant reading disability, but I discovered a nonverbal IQ of over 140 in his school records. I put him into a discussion group focused on non-academic concerns of gifted kids, and he quietly attended for the rest of the year, probably affirmed in a way he had never been. These students and others taught me to look broadly at "high intelligence" and to appreciate the reality that it may be masked by mild or serious learning disabilities.

Sweaty

His mom told him to assert
himself
to get
what she did not
(so he does)
this large
sweaty
one
whom we try to help
with hygiene and tact
(so that he can go
on the most recent trip
he has won)
who has grandiose plans
and speaks with largest words
whose distractibility
and disability
and huge emotions
preclude concentration
rob him of grades
though he tests well
and qualifies
(and needs to tell them)
is lonely
and needy
he stops in
every morning
and is too much
(for most).

Sweaty

He was not quiet in his group. Demeanor, mood, and a strong physical presence made this young man a force to be reckoned with from the moment he arrived and routinely announced events of his life. Many of the events were positive; he regularly and successfully pursued competitions involving essay writing, business plans, and citizenship proposals. He talked about how his mother cheered him on.

It was difficult to ascertain whether his bravado reflected a lack of interpersonal intelligence, a disability, insecurity, a difficult life, or simply poor impulse control. Other group members mostly sat silently while he talked during meetings, giving him uncompassionate attention. Then I would "go horizontal" with my questions, asking others to chime in about what this talker had said. Or I would bring them back to the topic of the day, which I could rely on to redirect the group when needed. He was confusing to his peers—and to me. According to his school data, he was quite intelligent but had some weak subtest scores. I wish I had understood more about his data; I hadn't had much training in assessment yet. But I knew it was important for him to be in the group.

This boy is a reminder of how difficult it is to generalize about "gifted kids." They don't all have solid social skills, nor do they always have those skills modeled for them. They don't all look neat and tidy. Some are obnoxious. Some desperately seek approval and affirmation, are highly focused on themselves, and are unable to step outside of their own emotional world to observe others' nonverbal responses. I wish I could have been more effective in guiding him, although he had my active support both in and outside of the group. I found myself defending or attempting to explain him to teachers, and I realized belatedly that he probably had an attention-deficit problem.

When I did a follow-up study of his graduating class, he was one of only a few academic underachievers who responded. He had not survived his first year of college—too much television, absent from classes, risky behavior. He said he had learned difficult life lessons. I contacted by phone the underachieving classmates who had not responded and found that 52% of these former underachievers had had four years of college, 41% had done better academically than in high school, and 26% had become achievers. Even 45% of the most "extreme" underachievers had gone to college for four years. However, he wasn't among them. Findings like these argue that low achievement may reflect developmental struggles, but it seems that these kids can often put peer and family issues at arm's length during the next stage of their lives so that they can accomplish developmental tasks and move ahead. I wonder how he turned out.

The Credit

When they discovered
he was short an English credit
his last semester,
his counselor called
the others together.
How could this brilliant one
not graduate on time?
Impossible.

The principal
came to me and said,
"You were an English teacher.
Figure it out."
I made an independent study
of classic short novels,
for which he was to give me
a weekly journal,
responsive.
He recognized the gift.
A memorable experience for both of us.

In the end
I kept a copy
(He said I could)
to remind me
how an ad hoc differentiation
gave his non-linear head
and mine
rare, long inspiration,
and how a nimble principal
knew how to punt.

The Credit

Educator rigidity can stifle more than just the most creative students; not encouraging appropriate academic risk-taking can constrain the most perfectionistic students as well, limiting their options. Program rigidity can similarly limit intellectual and artistic exploration. Curriculum differentiated for gifted students does not mean simply less guidance, more quantity, more homework, more pressure, and a faster pace. While each of these adjustments may be appropriate for some or many gifted students, they are simply not suitable for everyone. Yet Advanced Placement courses often constitute the entire "gifted program" in high schools. Programs, per se, also often do not go beyond honors classes in middle schools. Needs vary—creative outlets, opportunities for independent study tangentially related to school curriculum, cluster grouping, gates opened for passionate interests, and an affective curriculum that pays attention to social, emotional, and career development, for instance. These constitute "differentiated curriculum" as much as do high-powered, accelerated classes. When teachers and administrators are not knowledgeable about, sensitive to, and observant of high-caliber students' intellectual, expressive, and affective concerns, some may fall through the cracks of the system, depressed, stressed, and feeling lost.

It was easy to cluck tongues over what happened here. What a joke, among those who knew, that he was a credit short—and in English, an area of particular strength in him. I knew him because of his faithful discussion group attendance, his music, and an earlier stint on a Future Problem Solving team. His extremely non-linear, non-sequential mind was valuable on that team. He probably did not double-check course offerings and credits or do other "accounting" in his heavy-traffic head. His mother mentioned a divorce and his brother's moving away to college. Maybe those factors contributed to his flat affect and distance, even when peers in the group tried to engage him. If they knew about the credit dilemma, teachers probably were unsympathetic. But if they had ever experienced depression, they might have viewed it differently. He was able to get out of bed each morning and come to school, but beyond his music, I wondered what engaged him. He seemed anxious. He would be leaving soon for college himself.

I'm glad this worked out. The carte blanche inherent in the principal's directive was the key. My approach to teaching literature had involved open-ended reading and frequent writing. Gifted students didn't necessarily do more and do it faster, but they knew I'd be excited about insights, creativity, nuanced language, and clarity. They could think as deeply and as strangely as they wanted to. I had been missing the English-teaching stage of my career and was more than happy to put a familiar approach to use when this boy needed a credit. His insights were indeed amazing.

Yearbook Photographer

He joined the yearbook staff
when an antique camera
in the attic
seemed like a destiny,
went quickly from novice to expert
in his darkroom,
won us prizes,
worked for the paper
in the small town
and then in the big town
and for us,
wrote wonderfully,
too,
and everyone asked much of him,
a heady time,
went off to school,
was ahead of them there,
kept his jobs,
dropped out at 19,
depressed,
burned out—
two years
before a return
for something else
and room to choose
to open up the camera case
    again.

Yearbook Photographer

He did not appear to be light-hearted, and perhaps because of this I paid particular attention to him. Kids like him played a role in establishing my future research direction, but I didn't know that then. He was in a particularly easy-to-teach, socially and linguistically adept, highly invested (and greatly appreciated) group of about six to eight that year. Because I knew them outside of English class through yearbook activity, we became well-acquainted, and I was able to follow their personal and academic development fairly closely for their last three years of high school. Good things happened for this one, particularly in writing and photography, and he indeed had amazing talent. But he never obviously called attention to himself. For a while, he dated one of the girls in the group, and they were a good match.

He taught me, without words, about overkill—the kind that teachers and coaches and even parents may be guilty of, and the kind that talented students may pay a price for. He seemed self-driven in high school, but we clearly took advantage of that in meeting needs related to the school paper and yearbook. Since then, I've seen young athletes burned out by middle school, musicians leaving their phenomenal craft in their twenties or experiencing the physical toll of repetitive movement, and highly academic students needing to take time off. When I notice these, I remember the impressive adolescent in this poem.

He majored in psychology in college, and that made sense when I thought about it. But he did eventually use the camera again. In fact, several years later, when I began to see his name under photos in state tourism literature and in scenic calendars, I contacted him to congratulate him. He had an extraordinary sense of how to capture and call attention to natural light. Colors were always rich, and compositions exquisite. He was doing well. He lived near a national park, was married, and was satisfied. I could see him smiling in his email.

Only by Grace

Only by grace
is he still in school,
this tight spring,
wound by ethnic differences
and parents
who blame the system
and the culture,
not their lack of limits,
who agree only about
the problem:
he who screams
and schemes
in creative ways
to be stopped.
In second grade
out East
tests showed the gifts.
No more.
Drugs
have leveled the data.
He stays in our group,
where he doubts he belongs.
When we meet one-on-one,
we start by
speaking of where
his intelligence shows.

Only by Grace

This boy didn't fit the stereotype of bright, academically driven, conscientious, highly focused Asian students. Not at all. Teachers and counselors were quite aware of him in that middle school. Many blamed the parents, but I felt sympathy for them. I assumed they had deep frustration about where to begin to unravel whatever had led their only son to be so perpetually in trouble, belligerent, and angry. His eyes flashed easily—even in our group, which he attended until he was expelled from school. The others listened with rapt attention whenever he talked. There was something fascinating about him, but this was middle school, and neither they nor he had the wherewithal to make sense of his flailing. There was talk among teachers that the parents were considering a military school.

He'd earlier had high scores on group intelligence tests. Not all children with behavior problems like his demonstrate their ability on group tests. Too many aspects and issues in their lives may preclude their ability to focus—or their willingness to show what they know on such tests.

Whenever I was providing programming, I annually sifted through data on incoming students to find gifted students who had moved in after the typical "identification years," or who had become "ungifted" when they failed to perform as expected, or who had simply never been identified. I also wanted to find current underachievers, since I believe lack of motivation for academic work can reflect any number of developmental, emotional, family, and learning issues. I hoped to provide program components that would engage these students and connect them to others. I wasn't surprised to find many who, in elementary grades, had had standardized test scores in the high 90th percentiles—at least on some of the subtests, and sometimes on most of them. Obviously, something had happened between then and their later school years. In my studies of underachievers, I found that developmental task accomplishment sometimes leads to motivation for academic work. When two or more milestones are in place (for example, finding career direction, developing a significant relationship, achieving an appropriate level of autonomy, establishing a sense of identity, or resolving conflict with family), life becomes much more positive. Sometimes this happens by the end of high school, sometimes during college, sometimes much later.

The struggle of the boy in this poem with identity development was probably compounded by differences between his and his immigrant parents' level of acculturation. His response to his situation affected how he responded to *all* authority. Yet his school behavior and impassioned comments in his discussion group probably represented action, not paralysis. He was "working through it" and probably continued to do that. I do hope that he accomplished appropriate developmental tasks over the next several years, figured out how to *be* in his world, and was able to get important needs met, including through education.

About Junior High

Beautiful Carrie told about geeks
and how she didn't have a boyfriend
all through junior high.
Envied Susie wanted only James
and got him.
Craig moved here in eighth grade
and was lonely.
Troubled Josh wanted teachers
to have control
because he didn't have any.
They talked about
how they studied the "in"-crowd,
gauged males by bench-press rank
and females by bra size,
and were moody
during junior high
in our best discussion yet.

About Junior High

My groups, regardless of school venue and population, are always age or grade stratified. I reason that, even though social and emotional maturity probably varies greatly among classmates, and even though ability level also varies, group members typically interact with age peers on a daily basis. They are also likely to be dealing with similar social and emotional developmental concerns. Even when someone is not as physically developed as most others (or perhaps more physically developed than most) or is more or less socially mature than others, the need to manage the social world in school at their age or grade level is a shared issue. Even with grade-accelerated gifted kids, I prefer that they be in groups geared to social and emotional concerns with age peers. In general, I recommend that gifted kids be grouped together for small-group work.

Early every year in my sophomore (grade 10) discussion groups for gifted kids, one session focused on "junior high" (grades 7-9). When I'd announce that particular topic (I never revealed topics ahead of time), I learned to expect a collective "Oh! Those years were *awful*!" It was always an energized, emotional, open, and candid discussion, and thereafter each group typically was at a new level of group development. Members learned that there was a great deal of commonality among them related to the junior high experience. I recall that one referred to that school level as "a black hole." Others described "not knowing who I was" and "being so worried about what everyone else thought of me." The sophomore year felt quite different for them. I wasn't surprised, since teaching sophomore English had convinced me that general population sophomores were not only ready for serious literature, but appreciated being pushed ahead with writing, thinking, and awareness of societal issues.

I loved the "junior high" discussions. We'd chuckle at tales of awkwardness, embarrassment, and naiveté. We'd soberly consider how some had replaced achievement motivation with preoccupation with social connection. Some would mention loneliness, heartbreak, conflict with and between adults in the home, behavior problems, relocation, and irritation at not having differentiated instruction. They learned expressive vocabulary and skills, which would serve them well in future school, employment, marital, and parental interaction. And they were glad that they were in high school, not junior high.

Trying to Fix Himself

He doesn't sleep much—
is into Eastern things now.
Younger siblings
absorb family attention
and make noise.
There's money enough,
but also quiet chaos,
his basement bedroom
still unfinished.
He tries to sleep on couch cushions,
concentrates on science areas
to gain access,
but his dad works late
and doesn't like noise.
He smiles in the halls
because no one likes depressed people.
He volunteers to clean the physics lab
because that is a comfortable place
with a man to talk to.
He never speaks of the gray wash
that he feels
because it is his job,
he says,
to figure it out.
They do not know
how much he needs
a room of his own,
and he is afraid
because he is taking so long
to fix.

Trying to Fix Himself

During the years I directed the high school gifted program, I was aware that some of the students were struggling with depression. Some were on medication for it. Others had not sought help, believing that it was their responsibility to figure themselves out. When it seemed situational, I sometimes viewed it as a paralysis of spirit in the midst of high expectations and high-achieving parents, or as a response to significant change and loss, a manifestation of disappointment, or a sense that difficult circumstances would never change for the better.

I made sure that we talked about depression once during each first-year group's existence. As an English teacher, I had taught Rolvaag's *Giants in the Earth* for several years, a hauntingly credible portrayal of depression during the pioneer era. Each year, some of the brightest students, in their weekly response journals, mentioned that they could relate to the woman who felt desolate on the vast prairie. Therefore, when I began my work with gifted students, the discussion groups were intended to offer a place to talk about stressors, scary feelings, disappointments, frustrations, and loss. Students were always attentive when I provided basic information about depression, or invited a mental health professional to talk about it, or showed an appropriate video followed by discussion. No one ever revealed suicidal thoughts at those times, and few revealed that they were currently depressed, but usually some explained that they had experienced it previously. Some came to talk privately about it, and I accompanied them to their counselor's office if I sensed that they needed more than I could provide as a teacher.

One day I noticed the gray pallor of a girl who came early to her group and sat gloomily, waiting for the others. I said, "You don't look so good," and she proceeded to tell me how angry she was after a classmate's death, even though she hadn't known him personally. She said, sorrowfully, that not long after the death had been announced, "Everything just went back to normal here. That's terrible!" Others had arrived by then, and we continued to talk about their lingering responses to the tragedy. She and two others articulated carefully what depression was like and connected it to feelings of anger, sadness, and hopelessness. The boy who is the subject of this poem was in that group.

Media reports periodically confirm that depression is not unusual among adolescents. There has been no empirical evidence that it is more or less likely in gifted teens than in others, but even if the prevalence is "just" similar, adults who work with them should be alert to it.

When the Advocate Died

His teacher gave this fifth-grade legend
Lamb's Shakespeare,
talked to the class
when he was absent,
hoping they would let him
be a boy with them,
accelerated him to seventh.

That year I met his mom,
just then divorced.
She understood
and pushed until she caused a program—
a soft and gentle, earnest mom
with furrowed brow,
his advocate.

I met him when he entered
English class in tenth,
disturbed by imperfections,
never smiling,
hyper-alert,
and young and tense.
An off-the-scale IQ, they said.

That year I met his dad.
A rigid, severe, former Army man,
who had the future mapped,
he had remarried, and
it's said
the son had cut all ties.

Then Mom was killed
at 8 a.m. one day
(an icy curve).
They took him out of English.
My heart stopped when I heard.
He came back the next day—
said he might as well.
A flat affect forever,
and no one knew the words to say.

68

When the Advocate Died

Bad things can happen to gifted kids, just as they can to anyone else. They can experience family upheaval, terrible accidents, the death of loved ones, bullying or other social problems, conflict with significant others, and unexpected changes and loss—as this boy did. When he left the classroom that day, I turned my back to the class and struggled to compose myself. I knew that the reverberations of the tragedy had now begun. The other students were told later, after the death had been confirmed. I've often wondered how life unfolded for him over the next decade and beyond.

Trauma is certainly not limited to war or abuse or the death of someone close. It may be related to marital tension at home; witnessing violence, including being a bystander of bullying; being a target of bullies; natural disasters; or experiencing extreme rumor spreading or peer exclusion. The emotional distress of trauma may come from one event, or it may come from extended horrific experiences. Post-traumatic stress can be reflected in feelings of anger, humiliation, powerlessness, distress, and despair; extreme emotions and emotional confusion; lack of trust; a frantic need for control; self-harm and self-medication with substances; isolation, withdrawal, and depression; and interpersonal difficulties. Overexcitabilities and perfectionism may add a layer of intensity to gifted individuals' responses to these experiences.

Teachers, athletic coaches, employers, mentors, and directors in the arts may actually spend more focused time with students than parents do, sometimes with sustained contact over several years. Those relationships give school personnel opportunities to be supportive. It is important for them to remember that grief does not have a beginning and an end. There is no specific duration, after which someone should "be done with it." Children and adolescents may experience intense, long-term grief, even though it may not be displayed or expressed. "Rescuing" them may curb important grief activity—may in fact reflect the rescuer's discomfort more than the bereaved person's need. Adults' telling of their own experiences with tragedy or invalidating intense feelings with "You'll feel better soon" are not as helpful as they are assumed or intended to be. Instead, respectful, caring adults can use statements that validate sadness and confusion and allow the child to experience the feelings ("This is a really rough, sad time for you." "It's okay. People cry when they're sad." "It makes sense that you're angry."). They can approach a sad student with a simple "How are you doing?" or "I'm so sorry about your dad." Having permission to feel and express emotions, step back from heavy assignments for a time, and lean on someone for support can help children heal. Healing may take a long time. How a significant adult responds may long be remembered as a key.

Wounded

I read his papers first,
the sensuous words
resonating—
a rarity at 15.
This one gave eye contact
without smiles,
put it on paper,
starred in the plays,
sang brilliantly
to Mother's applause,
made Dad wince
with these gifts
that weren't his
or were.
The director asked
if I would speak
to this wounded
golden boy
about the alcohol.
He pushed the brightest girl
away,
said he couldn't love girls,
was a lush
for the one year
he lasted in college,
found himself
and a lover
later,
an emancipated connection
to the father
finally.
This wounded one
might make it.

Wounded

We all were shocked to hear that this prodigiously talented graduate had not completed his first year of college. He was one of the most gifted students we could remember. What had gone wrong? Probably only two or three teachers had known about his alcohol problem. It is likely that none of us knew about his sexual orientation. When he looked me up a few years later, he had just finished a year of college and seemed happy, clearly more relaxed than he had been in class. He talked about his struggles during and after high school. I had thought I knew him well, but I had not recognized the angst, and that lack of awareness bothered me when I learned of his difficulties. Certainly he wasn't the only homosexual student I taught then or later, but he probably had something to do with my later deciding to conduct a study of the school experiences of gifted individuals who are gay, lesbian, bisexual, or transgendered.

What I learned in that qualitative study of 18 gifted GLBT young adults was that half had wondered seriously about their sexual orientation before leaving elementary school, and all but one of them was convinced of their orientation by grade 11. Almost all of the 88% of the participants who had experienced severe depression during the school years reported being suicidal at some point. None had been open with teachers about their distress, and only 29% had discussed being suicidal with parents. Of the 78% who received counseling, 79% considered it helpful. Coming out did not occur until after leaving home for 72%, perhaps when the threat of family abandonment mattered less and perhaps because of, in the words of one participant, "the suspicion that…you…will not be readily accepted by family, friends, and education." Most parents "came around" eventually with support. But real and perceived danger had lurked for 65% of the participants, and for 41%, it was school that felt unsafe. A few of the latter reported that teachers and coaches openly harassed them or spread rumors about them.

Participants emphasized that, in every classroom, there are students wondering seriously about sexual orientation, fearful about the future, concerned that the dream career may not embrace them, unable to freely explore relationships, sad to be "dishonest" with their parents, quitting some activities out of fear and gravitating toward others that embrace diversity. They said that teachers should have zero tolerance for slurs related to sexual orientation, should note GLBT figures in history and literature, and should not assume that references to heterosexual relationships resonate with all students. One said that he wished there had been more gay role models when he was in middle and high school—as there have been since then. Another, who said he had "given 150%" to everything in order to "compensate" and as self-protection, wished teachers had noticed his stress and encouraged him to relax.

Brian and Christi

Even when attendance
at the lectures after school
lagged,
Brian and Christi,
handsome eccentrics,
were pleasantly there.
Even when the poetry time
was changed
and beat the sun up,
they came,
ready with their metaphors,
juice, and rolls.
They were two of the most gentle
that year,
with interests
in sync.
I shouldn't have been surprised
at his graduation coffee
when they stood together,
smiling,
and said
they had been going out
since April.

Brian and Christi

Christi's poetry reflected her kindness and gentleness. I hadn't expected her to join the group, but she did, and her work was solid. Brian's was completely outside of the box—initially edgy and cryptic, but gradually becoming more tender and straightforward—even romantic. All of the poets tried new styles and various forms, and therefore I didn't read anything into Brian's changes. Obviously I missed some nuances in the interaction in front of me. I learned a lot from those spunky writers. Their poems reflected who they were.

The beauty of the early morning poetry meetings was that we were entirely about expression—without competition or evaluation. My years with this activity convinced me, even more than the discussion groups did, that being encouraged to express the inner world—as it interacts with the outer world—allows students to make sense of themselves and move forward more confidently in their social, emotional, and even career development.

One of my themes when I speak formally about incorporating attention to social and emotional development into programs for gifted students is that most or all program components inherently have social and emotional dimensions, with opportunities to "process" whatever is felt, experienced, accomplished, or not accomplished. After a practice for a competitive activity, a director/leader can ask open-ended questions to encourage reflection and develop expressive vocabulary and skills: "What was it like to wrestle with changes in the rules?" After a theater or music rehearsal, a practice session or lesson, or an athletic event, one question might be "What were you feeling when I was pressing you to ratchet it up a notch?" Or "What was going on in you when she argued with you about that line?" Gradually, such questions can become normalized so that self-reflection is a given, equal to measurable productivity in value.

Brian and Christi experienced an extra dimension, probably not so unusual in extracurricular activities. Someone once told me that it is more important to find *something* to love than *someone* to love, since the passion for the former can last a lifetime, and finding someone to love may happen in connection with it. I don't know if Brian and Christi's relationship lasted, but they found each other through an activity that they had both gravitated toward. Relationships often happen in that order.

The Nicest Girl in School

They told her at seven
that her mother would not live
to see her graduate.
She made an early connection
between the pregnancy
that birthed her
and the onset.
She defended her mother
against tension
that made seizures.
She made up for the sister,
who made normal childish demands.
She did not stray far,
took care of chores and clutter,
was robbed of childhood,
robbed of conversation
with a mother then.
Many angers needed words
in the nicest girl in school.

The Nicest Girl in School

I remember the day that this girl told us about her mother and her sister. Hers was a lovely middle school group, with each bright, serious student leaning in expectantly when someone else spoke. Each session had a new focus, which I typically introduced briefly at the outset. They eagerly dived in, regardless of topic. They had met for several weeks, and they had moved from preoccupation with grade points and bravado to allowing themselves to be vulnerable. No one criticized, no one argued, no one spoke loudly, and no one interrupted anyone. It was an ideal group. They had bonded and found common ground related to growing up.

Since this girl usually didn't say much, the group seemed surprised when she started talking that day. The topic was probably stress, or siblings, or worries, or fears. She talked at length, and the rest of us were silent. She was wistful, not sad, but it was clear that she carried a heavy weight. She chose her words carefully, speaking discreetly, while at the same time allowing her peers to see her complexly. Someone said, after she stopped, that they'd never have guessed that she was sad and stressed. Others agreed.

This poem reminds me that gifted kids—or anyone—may not be what they seem. High achievers typically don't warrant concern, since they are motivated, help teachers and parents to feel affirmed, may generate smiles in those around them, and seem to be headed for adult success. In contrast, gifted underachievers may provoke concern or frustration in these same adults—if the latter are aware of the high ability. But some achievers' performance may belie social anxiety, fears, worries, discomfort, or perfectionism. Some underachievers' bravado or withdrawal may represent the same—including perfectionism. Each gifted child and teen is a story. Each can benefit from an opportunity to meet with highly able peers and a nonjudgmental, secure, non-voyeuristic adult who is not preoccupied with their performance and who can facilitate a discussion about social and emotional development. My guess is that this nicest girl benefited greatly by talking about her stress with compassionate peers she had learned to trust.

Guilty

And the jury of unequal peers
pronounces them GUILTY
for being
getting
having
doing so much
for such a good life
assigned penance for life
a life sentence
with no parole
sentenced to giving
they are not innocent
but the debt has long ago been paid
they know
but cannot say it
as defense
and the gate is shut
and the sentence continues
no one noticing
and no one worrying
because the burden
is invisible and
unspoken.

Guilty

Age peers, educators and other significant adults, and the public at large do not have a window for viewing the inner world of gifted kids. Without recognizing the social and emotional complexity of giftedness, some may consciously or unconsciously indict these children for "easy" gifts. Guilty as charged. Yes, the gifts are there. However, they may not be carried easily.

Some highly able kids actually feel guilty for these assets. Maybe it's because it gives them an easier relationship with their parents than their siblings have. Maybe it's because they are able to interact with and embrace classmates at all ability levels and feel compassion for those who struggle interpersonally. Maybe it's because, especially during elementary school, they already know most of the material being taught, and others do not. Maybe it's because a sibling, relative, friend, or other age peer does not have a comfortable relationship with teachers, homework, and school in general—and they themselves do. They may be aware of and actually witness extreme bullying and harassment of others at school, and they appreciate having good peer relationships themselves. They may see that a teacher or principal is a bully and feel guilty for having positive (or at least safe) relationships with these educators. In general, they may be concerned about the differences in ability that they see around them in school or at home.

Gifted kids who have uncomfortable or unsuccessful relationships are probably less likely to feel guilty. However, "difficult" gifted kids may feel guilt over contributing to family stress, given the likelihood, according to pertinent scholarly literature, that they have an extra layer of sensitivity—including to injustice.

Pertinent wisdom comes through life experience. Whatever gifted children and adolescents perceive, feel, or are burdened with, they may not be able to make sense of these experiences, since asynchronous development may limit their ability to comprehend social and emotional nuances. With cognitive development outpacing social and emotional development, they may also be wrestling with phenomena that they are not emotionally equipped to handle.

Underachievers

This homogeneous group
of underachievers
collectively prefer personal topics,
respond cautiously,
then passionately,
to the invitation
to express themselves,
articulate,
incisive,
from a young life of complexity
and introspection
from not doing the expected,
responsive to each other,
noncompetitive—
an easy sharing.
They read each other well.
They recognize and affirm
the hormones
openly and humorously,
take social risks and laugh,
have opted out of the race,
don't flaunt uneven grades,
but share them
with no shame.
They aren't used to being listened to
by adults.
They aren't used to no grades
and no product.
We will first enjoy the safety.
They could learn something
from my other group.

Underachievers

Regardless of school level, when I formed discussion groups from the list of interested gifted students, I typically didn't mix grade levels, but I did intentionally mix academic achievement levels, personalities, interests, cultures, socio-economic levels, and genders. One goal was to broaden students' view of the construct "gifted." Another was to broaden their appreciation of differences. Yet another was to help them become acquainted with others of high ability, discover commonalities, and feel more comfortable and connected within the classes they had together. Comments at the end of each group's year of meetings indicated that all of these goals were met at some level.

The year I wrote this poem, student schedules dictated that I couldn't mix achievement levels in two back-to-back sophomore groups. One would have to be all academic underachievers, the other all achievers. The underachievers bonded quickly, talked readily, laughed easily, and shared serious concerns comfortably. The achiever group frustrated me, and the next poem will explain why. One day, I developed a strategy for addressing some issues that I believed were holding the achievers back as a group. I talked with their geometry teacher, some of whose students came to the achiever group directly after that class, and asked if she would mind dismissing them 30 minutes early the next week—just one time. I told her I wanted to mix the two groups to see what they could gain from each other. She smiled and said, "*Take* them!" She said that this group of achievers dominated the quieter students, were hyper-competitive, argumentative, and a challenge.

The following week, the achievers joined the underachievers halfway through the latter's hour. They then stayed for an extra half hour and discussed their experience. I had asked the underachievers to pick the topic for the day (breaking a pattern, since I usually chose it myself and often prepared a brief activity as a discussion catalyst). One suggested drug use during adolescence. No one opposed it, and I decided not to object. When the achievers arrived, they were fairly quiet, seeming uncomfortable at not being in charge. The underachievers then outdid them—not afraid to speak candidly, with feeling, with respect for each other's opinions, politely, gently, and with chuckles now and then. After the underachievers left, one achiever said, "Wow, they can really talk about things." The achiever group proceeded to explore their collective realization that they themselves were not as conversant about growing up, exploring identity, and peer issues.

I also noticed that the achievers were surprised to see who was in the other group—the underachievers who were identified as gifted. My guess is that they had previously not considered the "scruffiest" of them to be in their league.

Achievers

This homogeneous group
of high-stress achievers
preferred global issues,
debate-style,
half of them excelling
at verbal dominance,
increasing volume and tempo,
ignoring the shy ones,
missing the cues,
escalating the tension
gleefully,
competitively,
alternating one-up moments.
Only the bell stopped them.
Now there is
little competition
when we talk about
perfectionism,
stress,
anger,
depression,
learning styles,
relationships,
success and failure.
Here they are equal
and vulnerable
as they define themselves,
share humanness,
find commonalities
unexpectedly.
They learned something
from my other group.

Achievers

I decided to take another risk as I prepared for the joint meeting of the two contrasting groups (described in the commentary for "Underachievers"). I had been unsuccessful, to that point, in moving the achievers into noncompetitive expressive language about development—the kind that might help them stay married or partnered someday, be parents who could communicate well with their children, and be colleagues who could coexist comfortably in the workplace. I wondered how to combat what I perceived as arrogance and entitlement. Actually, arrogance was usually a topic once in the life of each group, but I wanted this group to *experience* something before we talked about it formally.

I knew that some of the highest standardized test scores of the two groups were in the underachieving group, since I had checked school records when they entered high school. So I carefully created a graphic that gave the range and mean of IQ/ability composite scores for each group. Sure enough, the underachievers trumped the achievers. I enlarged the graphic and held it up after the underachievers left. The most dominant achievers looked stricken.

The next week, I met with the underachievers, whom I had not yet debriefed. They felt good about the previous week's discussion. I showed them the graphic, but they talked about it only briefly. They mostly focused on their impression that the achievers didn't have a sense of humor.

I don't recommend generalizing these "findings," based only on these two groups of eight or nine students each. However, these poems remind me of the dramatic differences between them, as well as that the "experiment" seemed to be a watershed moment for both groups. The underachievers had new appreciation for their own individual and collective personalities and strengths. They had smiled quietly when their scores compared so favorably—as if they knew that the achievers were shocked at that revelation. In their group, the achievers talked more easily about growing up, about pressures, expectations, doubts, control, worries, and concerns about the next stage in their lives. The next summer, after four of the achievers won a component of the national Future Problem Solving competition, one commented that his experience in discussion groups, especially the memorable combined session, had changed him. He actually chose not to pursue an Ivy League school in favor of a small, music- and humanities-rich liberal arts college in the Midwest, where he excelled, pursuing his talent and intellectual passions. One of his English professors later told me that he once wrote about what he had learned "in group."

Presentation by Dr. A

You could've said anything
on that subject
(SEX)
and they would've been grateful
because maybe you're the first one
who's said anything
on that subject
certainly 60 mph
at school
seriously
with humor
just for them.

Presentation by Dr. A

Weekly after-school lectures were an important component of the high school gifted program. The community was a regional medical hub, and there were also several institutions of higher education. The arts thrived. Experts were available in many areas. Some were retired and eager to come to speak. Typically at least 30 students attended, plus a few teachers. Some teachers whose courses were connected to the topic of the day gave extra credit for attendance. The lectures were open to anyone, providing good public relations with school personnel and yet clearly going beyond the regular curriculum. The material presented was different, varied, complex, and relevant. The audiences were largely from the gifted program, but most who attended were not the same students from week to week. I posted an announcement each week in the hallways, and students paid attention. I had been warned that nobody would stay after school for a lecture, but many did. Most students drove to school or used public transportation, making attendance possible.

We typically had several series during the year. A medical center volunteered 13 physicians who spoke about immunology, cardiology, and endocrinology, as well as teen pregnancy, eating disorders, depression, anxiety, biofeedback, and stress. Local historians addressed various topics, including Constitutional law, Eurasian politics, and the roots of terrorism. A retired theologian did a series on world religions. Artists brought slides of their work and talked about the creative process. Business leaders examined economic theory and application. Representatives of various cultures came to speak about belief systems and their history in the United States, including a group of American Indian drummers and singers from the state penitentiary. Panels of professionals who were applying their college degrees in the sciences spoke about their unexpected (e.g., hazardous wastes, water treatment, oil pipelines) careers.

I give this background as context for the importance of the presentation by Dr. A., a well respected psychologist. I had been told that he related well with adolescents and was an effective speaker—two crucial criteria for all lecturers. He was part of the medical series. The flier said he would talk about sex. Eighty attended—our best attendance ever—and we had to open the movable wall between two large rooms to accommodate them.

Bonsai Tree

When friends gave them the bonsai tree to warm
their house on moving, the directions were
to put it in the sun and water it
and pay attention to the form: first ponder,
then apply the clippers thoughtfully.
No problem. It would bloom, for sure, since she
knows flowers. Violets grow robust for her,
and wintering others from the deck works well.
Impatiens and begonia leaves take on
a different hue inside the house. She nurtures
well, she says, when they display their colors.

But this one, the shapely bonsai, seems
resistant. Two years now, and never once
a bloom. Religiously she adds green drops
to water, and it smiles and drinks them in.
The deep-green leaves look healthy, but the buds
that come dry up. Clearly a non-achiever.
It drops its shriveled buds.

                    Her husband wants
to throw it out: "It never blooms!" he says.
"Gardenia trees should bloom. It says so in
the book!" She sometimes wonders if he's right,
but never throws it out. The shapely bonsai
keeps instructing them, says, "This is who
I am. Look at the art of me; I fill
the canvas well. Look at the green. Don't change
the pot to bigger and don't clip me." So
they park their several artful interventions
for the moment, move it to the sun,
do water care and ponder the container,
look it in the eye and, still the pensive
parents, leave again and let it grow.

Bonsai Tree

Giftedness can be both asset and burden. It's hard to know how much the burdens have impact on poor academic performance. The gifted education literature has discussed motivation, relationships with teachers and peers, family system characteristics, learning disabilities, low expectations from others, economic status, and lack of home enrichment, for example, as potential contributors. The emphasis is often on figuring out key factors and then devising intervention strategies accordingly.

Underachievement is complex and multi-dimensional. Therefore, any strategy used in isolation is unlikely to produce change. In fact, I cringe when I hear a phrase like "to *make* him more motivated," sometimes assumed by frustrated teachers and parents to be the role of school counselors. I am doubtful that kids can be *made* to achieve, to care, or to perform. Yes, they can be bribed and the screws can be turned tighter, but the basic root of motivation to achieve is internal, and that's one reason underachievement isn't an easy fix. The factors mentioned in the preceding paragraph may each affect academic performance, but the phenomenon of low achievement likely includes social and emotional issues at some level. Hammering away with "If you only could…" or "You're so bright…" or "You're just lazy…" or "What's *wrong* with you?" likely will not be productive.

Underachievement in itself is not pathology. I tend to put underachievement into two categories: *won't* and *can't*. The latter may be the case when there is clinical depression, a significant learning or emotional disability, chaos or heavy responsibilities at home, or an inability to focus because of grief or extreme bullying, for example. Students may come to school depleted, distracted, worried, fearful, and unable to focus on learning. Pressure from adults is unlikely to change anything. I contend that being able to "stand beside" an underachiever, without judgment and without implying that academic achievement is *the* most important thing in life, may be crucial to the well-being of a low performer during a high-stress time. A good counselor can also help, focusing on the whole child or teen, not just academic work.

Development is one aspect of underachievement, a highly idiosyncratic phenomenon. Any number of elements may be issues for a gifted individual, almost all of them with implications for social and emotional development. Sensitivities associated with giftedness may contribute to anxieties or conflict or behaviors that preclude smooth transitions between stages. Significant struggling with any of these areas of development may affect a student's ability or willingness to do what is expected. It's hard to say whether the bonsai tree couldn't or wouldn't.

Awake at Night

They withdraw
young
with weird thoughts
and whirling images
from throbbing antennae,
absorbed in private fears
and fantasies
guarded deep
and deeper
in the centermost place,
wondering about death,
bothering with meaning,
feeling the marriage in their house,
tiptoeing around job tensions
that become theirs,
projecting ahead too many years,
wondering if they can do it well
enough,
awake at night,
the stage curtain open
on the actors and reactors of their play,
fearing they will never sleep,
and sure that no one feels
or thinks
as they do.

Awake at Night

Invariably someone in each discussion group revealed concerns about insomnia, usually in connection with the topic of stress. When I then asked if others had experienced problems with sleeping, usually the majority had. I'd quickly reassure those who always slept well that easy sleeping did not reflect lack of intelligence, and we'd smile about that. But we would indeed talk about issues related to sleeping. This poem reflects some of what I heard during those discussions. I typically said something about "dropping or closing the curtain on the day," and this usually resonated with the students.

I have experienced young children struggling with existential depression, thinking about spiritual matters, needing to make sense of the universe, wondering about death, exploring the deep loneliness that they feel when their concerns don't resonate with others, and assuming that no one can help them with what they explore at night and when they appear to be daydreaming in the classroom. I have also known adults who recall lying awake and worried during the early school years, not telling anyone, since they doubted that anyone would understand or that they themselves had the language to communicate their concerns.

If, as clinical professionals in the field of gifted education argue, rapid information processing and sensitivity to environmental stimuli characterize highly intelligent individuals, it makes sense that family and school tensions have particular impact on them. When sleep is not automatic when head hits pillow and a child tends to be anxious anyway, it also makes sense that fears might exacerbate the sleep problems. Being able to talk with someone who is both nonjudgmental and knowledgeable about giftedness and about sleep issues can be helpful. Talking with a skilled professional can normalize thoughts, feelings, and developmental challenges; can acquaint a gifted student with cognitive-behavioral approaches to alter thoughts and behaviors and diminish anxiety; and can help to develop expressive language for sorting out stressors.

Broken Yardstick

Periodically
another teacher would explain
about the eccentricities of his mom—
a saddle on the grand piano,
for one thing,
and insatiable reading
that earned her membership
in the Book Club
Sinclair Lewis might have written about
in this lakeless part
of lake country.

He was taller than most in ninth grade,
taller than his jeans
and more insolent,
misplaced in the B section
(of A and B)
of the English I taught,
where his antennae never rested.
The principal,
who never had control
of this little town,
had me witness
a yardstick
broken over this one's tall bottom
while humiliated hands held ankles.

After ten years
this handsome one
tracked me down
to say he owned busy equipment
and a Cadillac convertible
and squeezed overdue payments
out of those
who used to write him off.

Broken Yardstick

This story is a reminder of the impact of context on a child with high ability. This student's mother was recognized as a capable, creative, intellectual, well-read woman. Chances are, she had few equals in those areas, and her lifestyle certainly made her rare as well. Some of her peers were my faculty colleagues, and they were strong, capable, respected professionals.

My memory of the shaming "discipline" that was meted out is still clear. He was probably six feet tall at that time, and the situation struck me not only as horribly inappropriate and mortifying, but also shameful—for the principal. (I assume corporal punishment was still allowed there.) As an educator, I was embarrassed to think that this principal would stoop to taking out his frustrations in this way—frustrations related to kids who didn't behave as he wanted them to. To some extent, I understood the frustrations, since that "B" section of English was challenging for me, too.

I don't know if I said anything to the boy after the yardstick broke and before I turned away. (I saw the tears in his eyes and his tense, angry face and felt like crying myself.) But I do know that I continued to pay attention to him in class, making eye contact and wondering what was going on in his head. I don't recall him smiling in class. Maybe I didn't either—much. He didn't seem like the other boys, even though they were his friends, and he never misbehaved in class.

He went into the armed services after high school, saved his money, and then returned to his home area. Our conversation, a few hundred miles from where I had last seen him, was unexpected and astonishing. I remembered the families he referred to. I was grateful that he tracked me down.

When Kennedy Died

The day after Kennedy died
I asked the seniors
to write their thoughts,
and I found those papers
after twenty years
with hers on top,
the best by far,
and wanted to send it to her,
but had to settle
for sending it to those she left.
She died
not quite a year
after Kennedy,
a year when youthful promise
died.

When Kennedy Died

She was my best writer that year—my second teaching year—and my impression was that she missed nothing that was said, done, asked, presented, or discussed in class. Her mind was complex, and she was creative and insightful in what she wrote. I always looked forward to her compositions.

Within a year (maybe two) of Kennedy's assassination, three in her small graduating class had died—two in accidents and one gunned down far away. Just a few months earlier, two top academic students in the town where I had taught the previous year had also died—of cancer and heart disease, respectively. News of the deaths of these young, promising students was disorienting and unsettling. Those experiences were part of my initiation into the heartbreak of negative or tragic outcomes for students with great potential.

Much later, I found the set of essays in a file that I was sorting through prior to relocating. I'd often asked to keep, when I could, copies of remarkable essays. Because these about Kennedy were seen as sadly commemorative, they were in a separate file folder. There, on the top, was her beautiful, poetic essay. And, as I had done when my husband and I watched the President's funeral on a small, low-definition, black-and-white television in our apartment above the former movie theater on main street, I cried. Then I sent the essay to her parents.

Revenge of the Nerds

At the tenth reunion
one who used to be sickly
and drew airplanes
and never talked
came back handsome and straight
with his European bride.
A strange and brilliant one,
at the twentieth,
was recently married
and successful
in Washington.
An aerospace or nuclear-something
was there from California.
At the thirtieth,
one who used to be too serious
had lived all over the world
in foreign service
with his family.
More than one of these asked her out
in high school,
and she wouldn't go.
She wanted Tom, Dick, and Harry
because she was in high school,
had them later
and knew better.
Revenge of the nerds.

Revenge of the Nerds

Ask anyone who returns for a class reunion. High school social stature does not always last beyond graduation. In contrast, some who were nearly invisible, conscientiously studied, were not socially engaged, and were quiet in the classrooms have done well. Of course, there are many exceptions in both of these camps—unexpected difficulties and unexpected successes.

I have been struck by how many quiet kids who did not have stellar reputations academically have returned to the reunions of my own 90-student class with impressive accomplishments. One put an interest in cars into a rim-and-wheel company that was eventually sold internationally for multi-millions. One went into the military, found work later in engineering without a degree, and was not only successful, but built his own planes. One taught and then counseled in several exotic countries in international schools. Several became successful teachers. One ran a career-placement business for high-level professionals. One became involved in significant social service in Central America. One established a highly successful food manufacturing company.

I once officially reviewed a Canadian doctoral dissertation which focused on underachieving females. Among several interesting findings was the fact that though the underachievers often had seemingly more mature romantic relationships during high school, they were more likely to play subservient roles in them, with little autonomy and an apparent dependence on the boyfriend. The achievers, by contrast, generally had delayed serious romantic relationships, but if they'd had a relationship, it was likely to be fairly egalitarian. The underachievers asserted that they were independent, connected to peers, and distant from their mothers. The achievers tended to have more positive relationships with their mothers. Perhaps at a time when adult guidance was needed, the first group pushed away significant adults, including teachers, while the second group had more positive attention and guidance from those adults related to post-secondary plans and support.

Those findings may not relate specifically to the theme of the poem, but I mention them because they underscore that it is difficult to predict outcomes on the basis of what is apparent during adolescence, including academic underachievement and reticence. Individuals continue to develop, and underachievement may often be related to developmental struggles, resolved later. Low-profile students sometimes return to reunions with flair.

Whatever

She wondered
what a healthy family looked like.
A bonded sibling subsystem
had helped them survive
without normal schedules
normal foods
in normal quantities,
father's friends violating boundaries.

When I mentioned the school groups
as part of my agency job,
she wondered how anyone would know
who the kids of alcoholics were.
Her teachers had had no clue,
she said.

With a low-control,
good-humored,
unplanful style,
a victim mentality,
uncomfortable dependence
on an unavailable man,
a dependable designated driver
for poor-boundary friends,
checkbook problems,
tardiness to work,
vulnerability to siblings returning
and moving in
with dogs
and their baby to babysit,
she slept on the sofa,
couldn't fathom
separated siblings,
feared being alone.

A year of medication,
finding new models,
lots of practice,
some grief,
and she was ready to move away
and then return,
differentiated.

Whatever

It is important to consider that severe family dysfunction and lack of protection can happen even when parents and kids are quite intelligent, as was the case here. This poem, about an adult, is a reminder that adolescents in difficult situations are at risk for "stuckness" and poor outcomes, not only at that stage of development, but also later in life.

"Whatever," she would say after explaining something about her life, her past, her feelings, her difficulties. More than once, she said, "Everyone expects me to be there for them." Her role was firmly in place. This oldest sibling could not loosen and untangle the Lilliputian threads that held her. She could not imagine what a better life would look like, wondered how to change enough to get to work on time, how to say no to those who called during early morning hours, how to make a plan for getting the utilities connected again. She had a sense of what had contributed to her difficulties, and she struggled to find models to emulate and respectable values to embrace. She did find them, over time, and gradually resolved those issues.

I have met a number of individuals with backgrounds and personalities similar to the subject of this poem. My guess is that their teachers never guessed that such pleasant, smiling, joking, conscientious, intelligent, and high-performing kids were masking complicated and even neglectful home situations. Perhaps for them, like for this woman, school was their harbor. They could control achievement. Relationships with teachers and administrators they could also control—and probably with enough peers as well. Their teachers likely assumed that these students would move easily into adulthood, further their education, find a satisfying career, marry someone solid, and raise highly capable children. Some did do well, and some did not. Some wisely sought nonjudgmental guidance while exploring past, present, and future.

Siblings experience childhood and adolescence uniquely, each with different circumstances depending on birth order, presence or absence of important positive and negative influencers, unexpected and expected life events, and available role models. This woman's sister, for example, was influenced positively by a family that she became well acquainted with, and her developmental transitions were fairly smooth. Another advantage for her was that the subject of this poem was a stable, competent surrogate parent during their years at home.

Explanation

Alcohol removed her slowly
slowly
slowly
at mid-life
a dis-ease
for this shy one
with the mellow alto
in a world that was not hers
no clear direction
until a Mensa test
began the explanation
of the severity
of her handicap.

The third try
at treatment
worked.

Explanation

If sensitivities and Dabrowskian emotional, imaginational, psychomotor, sensual, and intellectual overexcitabilities are associated with giftedness, then it makes sense that some gifted individuals self-medicate discomfort and distress with one or more substances, including alcohol. This self-effacing woman had never considered that her high intelligence had contributed significantly to her distress and lack of social ease during the school years. I was amazed when she gave me some childhood and teenage details after she returned from treatment the final time. I'd had no clue about her past and present difficulties. Others, too, had not known about her problem with alcohol at mid-life. When treatment helped her to understand her life better, she moved forward more confidently, her family with her.

It is unfortunate that some adolescents look to alcohol or other drugs when they feel the gray wash of depression. Alcohol is a depressant, compounding the problem of depressed mood. Common assumptions in substance abuse treatment include that one's initial physiological response to alcohol may reflect the degree of threat of addiction. This might have something to do with genetic predispositions, of course, but reasons for using substances also play a role. How much is used, how much preoccupation there is with finding substances to use, when and where they are used, and how much the use affects work, relationships, and well-being are all of interest to someone conducting an assessment and treatment. When drug use begins and becomes problematic, and when developmental milestones are experienced under the influence of drugs, therapy must focus on filling social and emotional developmental gaps. When someone is addicted to a drug, the ability of the brain to "right itself" is affected. Repair requires time, commitment, and probably, assistance.

Like many other aspects of life, addictions may not be apparent to others, particularly outside of the home—at least until after considerable damage has been done.

Mentor Teacher

They thought she did
the eccentric bit
on purpose.
I didn't.
Genuine or not,
it let her be inept
at study hall supervision,
at turning in grades on time,
at matching blouse to slacks,
at driving,
at television trivia,
at gossip.
The kids in yearbook
made clever jokes
with her name
because they thought they should
and they had never known anyone
like her.
She was their brightest
and most learned
by far,
and she had chosen
teaching
at midlife
because she felt they needed her.
I, too, needed her.

Mentor Teacher

I have more than once made a mental note about the hypocrisy of significant adults in gifted students' lives who berate teachers for not understanding the need for differentiated curriculum and for not connecting well to the students. Too often, probably, those same adults would be loathe to recommend that gifted students with high levels of interpersonal intelligence, altruism, and creativity consider teaching as a career.

Teaching is a challenging career. The best are intellectually nimble, use their various intelligences to tailor their curriculum and delivery to children representing a wide range of ability, and are passionate about their work. They probably feel that they are contributing to the betterment of society—even in the least positive circumstances. The reality that many teachers do not remain in the profession past the first five years testifies to the challenges that teachers face. Perhaps it also reflects that bright, talented teachers may not receive support from family and society to stay in the field. There are undoubtedly many, many contributing factors.

Teaching is important work. We need the best and the brightest to be part of that work—not just for our best and brightest students, but for all students. Before young women had the array of career choices available to them that exists currently, the most talented often went into teaching, and a large number of them were eventually tapped to lead programs for gifted students. Many are now retiring or retired long ago, the latter including the teacher in the poem.

I was fortunate to teach with many bright men and women during my classroom and gifted education teaching years. Some nurtured their gifted students verbally and intentionally, some delighted the teachers' workrooms with their wit, some used creative approaches, some brought dramatic flair into their classrooms, and some spent their summers on grants in interesting places, eager to incorporate the learning into their teaching the next year. One highly intelligent colleague told me more than once that he appreciated having a career that paid him to keep learning. It was obvious that he loved his work and the students. A highly talented theater teacher said he turned his back on a successful acting career and had never regretted it. A physics teacher taught only inductively, sorely testing the perfectionists in his classes who wanted to be told what to know. An art teacher worked hard to make sure her students had opportunities to show their work and enter competitions. Like my mentor teacher, they contributed greatly to their school, their colleagues, and certainly to the gifted kids they taught.

Laughing about the Letter

Quietly, later,
she told me she had brought
a letter of recommendation
from Mother Teresa
when she came
for a doctorate.
I laughed,
not because it was preposterous,
mind you.

By then I was well acquainted
with her trip-hammer mind
and rapid intellectual processing
and quick conversational turns
and passionate professionalism.

I had to explain my laugh, of course,
because she had told me quietly.
I shouldn't have laughed.
It was because it fit so well,
and I wondered what
the committee thought
when they saw the letter.

Laughing about the Letter

This energetic former doctoral colleague has continued to delight me and others from our cohort at annual conventions. She is the consummate professional, respected, creative, outspoken, unselfish, and forward-looking. She is sensitive to people of color, herself certainly not resembling the pale Northerners who are probably 98% of the faculty and students at her institution. She brings her young graduate students to conventions, among them those from minority cultures. She guides them carefully, involves them all eventually in presentations, nurtures them expertly into the profession and into academia, pays attention to them, and brings them to dinners and social events so that we can interact with them. She models cross-generational professional generativity for the rest of us.

She has played a role in my professional life, too, with support, insights, avant garde presentations, and a serious, wise approach to professional issues. She contributes an international perspective inherently, but in reluctantly embracing her context, she also is a model for adaptation, without leaving heritage behind, a sturdy member of my still-close-knit doctoral cohort.

She is not a "gifted-at-risk" individual in the usual sense. She feels intensely, is seriously altruistic, cares deeply, and can be hurt as much as anyone else. But she is solid, resilient, courageous, competent, and confident. I thought a poem about her would be appropriate here, since the letter was so phenomenal that it needed to be kept under wraps. There might have been some risk in making it common knowledge. Others might then have misassessed her—and missed the fact that she has her feet on the ground, is not self-absorbed, and is certainly not arrogant.

A Teacher Running

he is a distance runner
pounding out depression
on asphalt and gravel
when the cycle comes around
predictably
patient and selfless
with the highly anxious
in advanced courses
checking out his perceptions
in the program office
but not after school
he takes
overworked antennae
to the pavement then
because there is no ease
in hypersensitivity
even at 40

A Teacher Running

I often thought, during my years in that school, how fortunate we were to have this bright, intense man on the faculty. He taught advanced courses in mathematics, and he was highly invested in the students. I became acquainted with him because he sometimes stopped in when he was concerned about students who were involved in the gifted program. He and I actually had annual conversations when girls, mostly, crumbled after two or three weeks in Trigonometry, Calculus, or Functions, deciding that they needed to drop the course. Facing new symbol systems in these courses, they had not brought in prior knowledge for support. In social studies, language arts, and the sciences, that wasn't the case. There, they had been able to envision the course prior to arriving in it, and many basic concepts were already somewhat familiar. Not so with higher math and foreign language courses, for instance.

This teacher would send me those girls for "shoring up," since I had their data handy and could remind them of their good minds and talk to them about Carol Dweck's work related to how young students think about intelligence. Dweck found that some view it as fixed—that is, someone either has it or doesn't have it. Others view it as malleable—that is, hard work and strategies help one conquer coursework and other challenges and, perhaps, "be more intelligent." It is a matter of performance goals versus learning and mastery goals, she concluded. She found that female students are more likely to ascribe to the former view, and male students to the latter, even though not all fit neatly into those categories, of course. When faced with frustrating challenges, students focused on performance goals might feel "found out"—not intelligent. These findings have implications for course selection and can be used by teachers and counselors as psychoeducational information to help gifted students make sense of self-doubt and not be crippled by it.

The above phenomenon comes to mind when I read this poem, but there was much more to this teacher than his being alert to student doubts. I was reminded often, then, of how crucial it can be for gifted students to have deeply committed teachers who not only are experts in their disciplines, but are also interested in individual students—paying attention to their eyes, their attention span, and their mood and adjusting teaching style and pace accordingly. This teacher was engaging, and he paid attention. In that high school, there were many strong math and science teachers, at least half of them female. In general, and perhaps partly because of the female models, bright girls generally took higher-level courses in those areas.

A Place with Color

he was a kid
with three other boys
who were his color
bright and full of promise
bussed across town
the only ones
with color
there
sat in the back
no teachers hugging them
joking
smiling
singling them out as promising
missed that
from the neighborhood
knew they shouldn't look
at pretty white girls

new prof
the only one with color
father
of a son
one of few with color
in a school
in the university town

will move to a place
with color
for the son

A Place with Color

I once spent two days consulting in a program for gifted students in a school that was 100% black. The school was struggling amid the economic downturn, reflecting the shrinking of the one-company community by more than half. But local schools were to be reconfigured, an opportunity for the program to reassess structures and curriculum. It had a long history, and it now had an opportunity to introduce new dimensions. I spent one day with the kids and a Saturday with the program teachers. My awe of all of them came home with me.

The teachers, I learned, pushed the students hard—prodding, hugging, celebrating, making college a clear expectation, investing in the future. I watched them do this before, during, and after their classes, as well as after school. My job that day was to interact with middle school students in cluster groups and, later, with high-school students during whole-classroom career-oriented events. I wished I could continue to experience their attentive seriousness and thoughtful comments.

This poem is not specifically about that experience. It actually was generated several years ago, when I read this university faculty member's personal recollection in a major counseling journal. He had written about the complex losses he experienced when he was bussed so far from home. But I thought about his story during the two days I spent in the schools described above. There would undoubtedly be challenging transitions for some or many when they eventually entered a culturally diverse university setting. But those transitions could be addressed and re-addressed prior to their leaving school. In fact, teachers did not assume, as they might have in an upscale, suburban setting, that parents and college advisors would sufficiently engage these students in this kind of preparation—or that preparation was even necessary. There was an urgency in the classes, with a both explicit and implicit emphasis on *why* they were being pushed so hard and so steadily. And the teachers did touch them, hug them, cajole them, and engage them. I could understand why the new university faculty member eventually moved.

Seven-Year-Old

He was having meltdowns
over errors on tests.
He said he was
a leader on the field
and everybody said so.
His dad had him do sprints,
timed him,
cheered him on
critically.

He was tense and solemn,
not wanting an ice cream cone
where we met.
He talked earnestly,
soberly,
how he needed
to be a leader,
that everyone looked up to him
and expected him to be one
so that others would stay focused
and calm
and not discouraged after a loss.

He wanted to stop melting.
We talked about
his "leader part,"
just one part of him,
how maybe he could
use it to stay calm
and not discouraged
after a loss.

I hoped for a second meeting,
one with Mom and Dad, too,
but it was one and done.

Seven-Year-Old

One of my biases, among many, of course, is that gifted children deserve to experience childhood as children, not as miniature adults. Regardless of their vocabulary level, or exceptional small- or large-motor skills, or insightful comments, they are indeed little kids. Socially and emotionally, they may be quite average. But even if they are precocious in those areas, too, they need to experience non-evaluated and non-competitive play, time to relax and unwind, time to be quiet, and time to figure out how they might spend their time instead of always having it structured for them.

A few years ago, a camp director who faced the demise of the camp after a long and complex history lamented that soccer had probably contributed to the steep decline in program enrollment. Instead of a camp being perhaps a single available summer experience, there was now a plethora of options for staying busy and involved. We talked about how summer camps in an earlier generation had encouraged campers to sit by a tree and meditate quietly on a topic or on nothing in particular, gather in the dining hall to sing camp songs with energetic young adults, create something artistic during crafts time, swim and canoe in a lake, and sit by a campfire and talk with camp counselors and other kids. Soccer, he said, didn't offer much in these areas. But, yes, it kept a lot of kids busy, and maybe that was a new value. He was going to make one last effort to incorporate other types of camp experiences at this place, and he had heard that I'd had a foreign language day camp in my former location. We tried it the next year, but few enrolled.

That conversation left an impression on me, and it came to mind as I talked with this little man at the ice cream shop, where I chose to meet with him after his mother called. I sensed that counseling was an uncomfortable thing for the family. Nevertheless, even if he didn't want ice cream, we had a good chat, and he articulated his feelings and perspectives very well. But he needed more.

Grief in the Queue

The favorite relative of the young boy dies,
and he loses his academic edge.
Anxious parents fear the future.
He needs challenge, one says.
He must be bored.
It is a catastrophe.

I hear it in her voice—
he may never be a good student again.
It is a breathless, long description,
with no request for guidance or opinion
after a presentation.

But it has been resolved, she says—
an accelerated school—away from home.
He will be challenged and regain momentum.

I gently ask what the boy thinks.
She looks at me oddly, then leaves,
and another parent steps up
from the queue.

Grief in the Queue

I use this extremely brief situation to underscore another basic tenet of my gifted education philosophy: students need more than speed and greater quantity. When differentiating curriculum, creativity and flexibility are usually positives. However, some teachers assume that a differentiated curriculum for gifted students is simply more and faster. Heavy labor may assuage parents' fears that their children will get into trouble if not kept busy, as well as teachers' concerns that parents think their children are not being pushed hard enough at school. Painstaking perseverance can be an asset in life, depending on goals and circumstances, but it may also discourage young learners. The amount of homework certainly needs to be developmentally appropriate, taking into consideration small-motor skills, social needs, temperament, need for play and physical movement, and rest. Parental anxiety, preoccupation with competitiveness, and grim evaluation of homework might not bear fruit. Challenge may be what is missing in some situations, yes, but it may also not be a critical *need*. Certainly it is not the *only* need.

Grief in children, as in adults, can take a variety of forms and vary in duration from child to child. Kids may not be able to "hold on to" grief for more than a few minutes, soon running outside to play after a moment of sadness. But that doesn't mean they are done with it. They also may not be able to articulate it and, given their sensitivity to the adults around them, may not want to "make mom cry again," instead holding in their sadness. Grieving may be delayed and come back in waves in both adults and children, and it may not look like what others perceive as grief. It may appear as anger and other out-of-control behaviors, for example. Child bereavement specialists and centers can be important resources. It is important to keep in mind that, in addition to death, grief can be associated with family relocation, dissolved friendships or romantic relationships, loss of innocence or "the way things used to be," and changes in family structure. Change means loss—something is left behind. Loss probably means grief, at least at some level.

In short, grief can affect cognitive ability, can be long-lasting, and can "come and go." Especially if not validated, it may feel crazy. Children can experience depression, which doesn't feel good at all. Challenge isn't the answer for all underachievers. I hope that this child was able to express his grief with a nonjudgmental adult—ideally a good counselor—in his new context. Psychoeducational information probably would be helpful as well, to normalize his feelings and perhaps his inability to perform well at that time. Of course, it is inappropriate for me to make such strong assumptions without being acquainted with this child. But the situation was presented to me in the context of a death loss, and I was troubled as I wrote the poem the next day.

Way Off the Charts

His dad wrote, from afar,
that he'd quit his job to parent full time
when they'd figured out that
Baby was over-the-edge smart.
Moments of repetitive movement,
when not occupied, had raised fears.

Dad crafted a keyboard so that
the non-stop explorer could manage games, search,
and have things for hands to do.
He was tall at two, and understandably clumsy,
so Dad made a safe place,
with colorful rubber squares as the floor.
They teased each other,
Dad making mistakes on purpose,
early-toddler giggling over multi-syllable words,
reading them, printing them,
playing with them in his mind,
spelling them backward, just for fun.

I suggested that they keep the media at bay,
remember his age, and let him be a child,
but it wouldn't hurt to document his development.
A clinician could validate the profundity.
Mom and Dad wondered about school and if
he would ever find a mind-mate.

Toddler grasped algebra instantaneously,
wrote lyrics and composed music with software,
remembered everything, sang well, had clear speech,
loved the chemical elements, surfed the Web.
Dad was often exhausted from non-stop interaction.
For resources and guidance, at three,
they found a Stanford program.
They did their best to let him be a little boy.

On a restricted listserv, they found a boy far away.
For a fifth-birthday surprise, families met,
boys made a connection, and they're in touch.
He began kindergarten this year,
and I'm waiting to hear how that has gone.

Way Off the Charts

Profound giftedness is not an area of special expertise for me, and I'm glad that this family made connections with appropriate resources. The little boy, like his parents, is charming, sweet, grounded, good humored, enjoyable to be around, respectful of adults, and not arrogant. The parents are doing their best to raise him to be socially and emotionally solid, loving to learn and explore, interested in others, optimistic, altruistic, and resilient. He already has these qualities, but of course his life has just begun, and complexities will undoubtedly test them all as his world becomes larger socially. In the meantime, he feels loved and enjoyed, I'm sure. It was difficult to measure his intelligence so early, since he played with the assessor, seeing how she would react when he turned answers upside down or gave one that he knew wasn't right. He was a toddler, after all, not understanding the gravity of it all.

Kids like him are so far out on the tail of the bell curve that those who teach and otherwise interact with them may be confused and uncomfortable—unless they self-talk their way into not being intimidated, not feeling inferior, and not needing to compete. If teachers, administrators, counselors, coaches, and directors can focus on the child and the child's needs, keep social and emotional development in mind, be reminded of the concept of asynchrony, recognize that they've lived longer than the impressive child has, respond with poise instead of amazement, and settle in for the conversation, they can be what the child needs them to be. Counselors, for instance, can't counsel effectively if they are unable to be totally present, appropriately objective, and not preoccupied with themselves and how they compare. I'm glad that "extreme ability" is now in the national standards for educators of counselors, since perspectives like these are important to include during training.

Will this boy find peers when he needs them? He might be without an intellectual peer in the entire country. Hard to say. He will have very few, if any, along the way. How he handles that will be key to his well-being. I'm optimistic, based on what I have seen so far.

Surprised

I noticed what books she responded to,
what statements she challenged,
what insights appeared in her journal
with detail and depth.

When I asked her to join
other best and brightest
to convince the powers
that we needed a program,
she was surprised
by the "gifted" term we used,
which reframed
what her brain did.

Her comments on the panel
helped inaugurate
what was long overdue.

Surprised

I, too, was surprised by this girl's impressive intellectual ability. She was pale and withdrawn on the first day of class. Her expression didn't change much during that semester and the next, but I certainly interpreted her sober face differently after her essays caught my attention. I didn't know much about her circumstances, but I guessed that money was in short supply. She always seemed surprised when she saw an "A" and an exclamatory compliment on a returned essay. I wondered if her good mind had simply not been noticed by former teachers or if she had previously not had opportunities to demonstrate her verbal skills on paper. Her work was on par with classmates who were well-known as excellent students, but she wasn't on the list of prospects for the proposed program. How had the school failed to identify her as gifted?

Identification checklists typically include behaviors that reflect comfort in the school culture and dominant-culture values, such as verbal ability and verbal assertiveness. Vocabulary is almost always on the lists, considered to be a reliable predictor, but English proficiency and/or assertiveness are required to demonstrate language-related strengths. The linguistic gifts of a child with limited facility in the new language will not be apparent when assessed in English. Low socio-economic background might also inhibit a child or teen from demonstrating verbal dexterity, and lack of print material at home might preclude vocabulary development. Demonstrating analytical ability also requires linguistic sophistication, and if highly capable students are not encouraged to take advanced classes in the humanities, they may miss opportunities to develop verbal dexterity for demonstrating critical thinking. IQ tests were originally intended to assess school-related abilities. Obviously, low skills in the dominant language mean some level of impairment in the classroom. Unfortunately, they may also preclude being involved in a gifted program with intellectual peers.

Perhaps more important and more pertinent here, however, is level of comfort with peers and teachers. Without social ease, unless there are opportunities to display ability on paper, a bright child like the one in the poem may be unable or unwilling to demonstrate intellectual curiosity, serious questioning, breadth of knowledge, wide-ranging or highly focused interests, and perhaps even energy, sensitivity, and sense of humor—all frequently listed in some form on identification checklists. Understandably, teachers need to base referrals on *something*, but students are at a disadvantage when life circumstances limit their sense of self, teachers' sense of them, and their ability to assert themselves verbally. After the panel mentioned in the poem, this girl's thoughtful responses were the ones teachers commented on most, perhaps because they were surprised to see her there, but perhaps also because she reminded them that the proposed program should reach out to kids like her and create components to engage them.

Prisoner of Love

She always had a serious boyfriend
like her sisters—
one through junior high
and one through high school
for keeps.
It was as easy for her
to speak of love
with glistening eyes
and poignant sighs
as to write extraordinarily,
because the family loved
dramatically,
redecorating her room
when she went to church camp,
giving headlined gifts,
keeping her close
in quiet, protected conflict,
her altruistic thoughts about careers
fighting only half-heartedly
against the loving,
eternally enmeshed,
and we were sad
as we anticipated
her graduation.

Prisoner of Love

One of the developmental tasks for adolescents and young adults is to figure out how to be separate from but connected to their family. Cultures and ethnic groups vary considerably in what *separate* and *connected* look like, but it's fair to say that adolescents' separate-but-connected self is always a "work in progress." Emotional connectedness, including being bound through ongoing, intense conflict even at great geographic distance, may delay or preclude differentiation of self. In this case, there was plenty of conflict, and it seemed always to be in the context of intense closeness.

I wrote this poem prior to learning about the family systems concept of *enmeshment*. When that and other therapy-oriented terms entered my vocabulary, I sometimes reflected on phenomena I had observed during my K-12 teaching career. This bright and beautiful girl's situation made better sense when I framed it in language associated with enmeshment, with terms such as *overconcerned, overinvolved, excessive togetherness, hyper-responsiveness, extreme proximity, extreme intensity, dependency, blurred boundaries, intrusion,* and *lack of separate personal space.* An extreme valuing of family cohesion may mean that movement toward individuality threatens a sense of belonging.

One counseling maxim reflects the idea that if something is working for all involved and not hurting anyone, there's probably no need to change it, even if someone inside or outside of the family perceives it as odd. It's hard to say if this was the case in the situation described in the poem. I know nothing about this young woman's life after graduation except that she did marry her high school boyfriend. If everything developed to her satisfaction, no problem, of course. However, from the perspective of the teachers, particularly the highly invested female teachers, she was pulled back and held tightly just as she was about to be launched. They were astonished by her decision to stay close to home. Actually, she had told me earlier in the year that she had never been without a serious boyfriend and that she was trying to view those relationships objectively, concerned that she was dependent on them. A theme of closeness and dependence had appeared now and then in her essays, too.

Teachers who are passionate and effective in their career are probably likely to invest in and be excited about students—maybe especially those with great promise. This investment helps teachers to continue and to feel good about their work, quite understandably. This poem reminds me that boundaries can be tricky and difficult to maintain—that is, knowing the line between a teacher's work and a student's life and future, the line separating teacher role from surrogate parent role, the line between "invested" and "too invested." Our sadness didn't mean that we had crossed the line, but it did provoke self-reflection. Parenting involves similar fine lines.

Sasha and I

Sasha upset her counselor
by procrastinating
until the eleventh hour
with college applications,
needing data and comments
from him by 3:00.
He told me
furiously
that he would not oblige her
on a Friday.

At 3:00
I gathered up
the recommendations
I needed for grad school next year
and ran home
and did the last part
and made it to the P.O.
to get Express Mail out
by 5:00
to be sure to have it there
by Monday.

Sasha and I

This poem is about how old habits die hard. I was smiling as I wrote it—the day after Sasha and I met our deadlines. I didn't appreciate her eleventh-hour insistence, but I understood it. I have a good sense of how much I can delay before applying rubber to the road, and I rarely miss a deadline. But I know that sometimes others are affected by my procrastination.

I can't speak for Sasha, and she and I never discussed this situation (or my habits), but I suspect that she was like me—and probably still is. She was heavily involved in theater, journalism, a job, and probably many other areas that I was not aware of. In her group that week, she had spoken about her fatigue, and I was sympathetic. One of her teachers had complained to me that the quality of Sasha's work was declining. He suspected that it was related to her having the leading role in an upcoming theater production.

Effective management of time and stress requires essential skills. I had recently demonstrated a meditation technique with each discussion group. I took the students step by step through compartmentalized relaxation and several minutes of near silence, encouraging them to check on the various "compartments" to make sure that they were still relaxed (feet, thighs, abdomen, shoulders, neck, jaw, eyes), and then, ultimately, to take a deep breath, observe the subsequent tingling in their fingers, and open their eyes slowly. This was a high-stress population, and I thought they needed this. They immersed themselves in it.

A few days before Sasha's application crisis, a debate student had rushed into my office after school and asked me to "do that stuff" with him again because he was "freaking out" while waiting for the next debate. We quietly did an abbreviated version (I benefited from participating), and then he thanked me, hurried out of the office—and thanked me again the next day. That was the day Sasha did almost the same thing—verbally. She had never stopped in to ask for anything, but she said she needed to talk. Her speech was rapid, her face flushed, her stressors many, and her frustrations evident. She talked for perhaps 10 minutes. Then she stopped suddenly and said, "That was *so* helpful. Thank you, thank you!" Then she left. I hadn't said a word—had simply listened, nodded, and murmured monosyllables as encouragement. I often refer to this experience when attempting to convince a school counseling graduate student (or a gifted education teacher or a parent) that just "shutting up and listening" can have a powerful effect.

Sasha was overextended, and maybe her assigned counselor "taught her a lesson" by refusing to help her with the application that day. She panicked, found me in my office, asked me for help, and I wrote a quick letter for her. We would have a chance to discuss procrastination at length in her discussion group. She wasn't the only student who could benefit.

At the Workshop

Six kids came
on Joe's last day in town
to teach the teachers
after being up late
for his party
to tell how they didn't fit
the stereotype.
Lisa couldn't believe
that teachers listened.
Derrick thought
they asked good questions.
Cory told one of them
he came reluctantly
but came because I asked.
Kim was as honest
as I'd seen her.

At the Workshop

When an organization invites me to do a workshop about social and emotional development of gifted kids, I often ask if it is possible to recruit six to eight students, fairly homogeneous in age, to be a panel. I ask for both achievers and underachievers, or just underachievers. This group was composed entirely of underachievers. I also usually ask for a mix of boys and girls, a range of high intellectual ability, and cultural and economic diversity. The students usually communicate more effectively than I about "what teachers should know about gifted kids." Simultaneously, I can demonstrate some small-group skills related to listening and responding, both of which are essential to developing communicative relationships.

This particular workshop was one of my first, and it happened to be in the district I'd left a year earlier to begin doctoral work. Some of the students from the groups I had facilitated were still in school, and a few had participated earlier in a similar discussion, with a principal observing, in which the students were in the teaching position. I'd invited a different administrator each year to hear about concerns of the gifted students and to be reminded of their developmental complexity.

Adults are not experts on kids' subjective experience of growing up. The kids are, and adults can learn from them. Adults may make assumptions based on clothes, hair, behavior, test scores, writing, oral expression, and academic and talent performance. However, what they see may not reflect the angst, concern, doubt, frustration, disappointment, shame, discomfort, and stress that gifted youth feel in various contexts. I chose these students with common adult assumptions in mind—and because I trusted that they had developed enough expressive language through the group experience to teach the teachers. I believed that they would appreciate a chance to do that.

I made sure, just as I did when facilitating groups at the school, to use open-ended questions (e.g., "What would you like teachers to know about kids like you?" "What are some teaching styles or approaches that you have appreciated?" "How much do you want teachers to know you personally?" "What is the most stressful part of school for you?"). I used statements to summarize what the students said (e.g., "Adolescence can be a challenging time." "Sounds like a rough semester."). When appropriate, I reflected feelings (e.g., "Sounds frustrating." "Makes sense that you were angry."). I made sure that my language and tone were thoroughly nonjudgmental. After all, I had asked them to come and be real. It took courage for them to do that. Adolescents can smell judgment from far away. It is much more productive to validate their feelings and experiences and accept them where they are—in the present—letting them figure themselves out through talking in the presence of peers and a stable, supportive, attentive adult.

Optimal Range

They say
there is an optimal range
in the intelligence quotient
where they can do
and be
whatever
if there is a green light
in the context,
the thrust,
and the trust.

Optimal Range

Giftedness is not always comfortable or advantageous. The literature about "severe" giftedness often includes discussion of extreme differences, especially pertaining to potential social difficulties when interpersonal and emotional intelligences don't match the intellectual, or if no mind-mate is available. Asynchronous development, especially during childhood and adolescence, is likely to be pronounced in profoundly gifted individuals. Abilities in various domains may also differ dramatically. When these individuals and the people around them can make sense of these discrepancies, perhaps they can embrace them, normalize them, focus on skill building when appropriate, and employ problem solving if necessary.

Early in my education and research activity related to high ability, I heard a presentation about "optimal giftedness." The speaker was referring to Leta Hollingworth's assertion, in the early 1900s, that anyone with even a "low superior" IQ like 120, specific intellectual strengths, internal motivation, and perseverance can probably enter almost any career and do reasonably well. The optimal range was 120-145.

I wrote the poem shortly after I heard that presentation. I have sometimes thought about the familiar joke that couples pray for "an average, *normal* child" during pregnancy. I have also considered that parents might pray for "ability that isn't too profound," since social and emotional ease may be difficult to accomplish "up there." Parents may be less inclined to ask for "average" in a talent area, I suppose, but extraordinary talent can indeed ratchet up parental expectations. Whatever the kind of extreme talent, the personality and needs of the child, as well as those of the mentor/director/coach/teacher, will affect whether there will also be extraordinary stressors associated with it.

Pertinent to this poem is the reality that there are no perfect assessments of ability and therefore no exact scores in the sense of absolutely determining level of intelligence. Too many schools use a single number as the cut-off point for identification for gifted programs. It is important to acknowledge an error range. Various factors can affect a score on either a group-administered or an individually administered (less likely, but of course possible) standardized assessment of ability: attitude, health, distractions, hunger, room temperature, cultural background of the assessor, size and attitude of the assessor, and willingness to "show what one knows," for instance. As much as programs want to avoid challenges during the identification process by relying heavily on scores and "certainty," relying on a single score at one grade level or stage of development is not wise. Schools are encouraged by national advocates to use multiple criteria (test scores being only one) and multiple sources of information when considering who might need and benefit from participation in a special program.

Small-Town Principal

Teachers don't like
intellectual principals
who know Latin and Greek
and prefer Augustine
and Aquinas.
Neither do other folks
in this stark place.
It is a lonely life
for principals
who grew up
on the fringes
and have few allies
in the rank and file.
This one knew theory,
but did angry things
with kids
who didn't care
and who did
what adolescents do.

Small-Town Principal

He wasn't my only intellectually gifted principal during my years in K-12 education. This one was in a small town, but school size wasn't a common denominator. Life circumstances often dictate where bright educators are found. I have no idea why this principal was where he was.

In this portrait, I wanted to capture the importance of finding a good fit in a career, not only with the "content" of it, but also with social and emotional aspects, including the kinds of personalities that gravitate to an occupation. There are certainly highly capable teachers in the ranks everywhere, and they were among my colleagues in this particular school culture, where teachers regularly attended most athletic events, meetings of the parent-teacher organization, plays, contests, and concerts. Since there was not much else to do in town, most school functions had a social dimension, sometimes with a social gathering afterward. Teachers knew each other well. Conversation was brisk, and substantive debates were not unusual in that eclectic group.

The principal was only rarely part of social gatherings, as well as of the usually brief but often intense teacher-workroom or lunch-time conversations. To some extent, professional boundaries made his distance understandable, but there was also the issue of fit. His behavior reflected what perhaps had been reinforced during his school years—a sense of differentness, low social self-esteem, a feeling that no one could resonate with his interests, and perhaps anger or even arrogance and a sense of judgment toward others.

I wonder what he expected in regard to fit when he pursued educational administration. Maybe he hoped to change school systems to be more accommodating of gifted kids like himself. What he probably did not reckon with is the reality that K-12 teachers are likely to be strong interpersonally and also entrepreneurially—in the sense of being able to sell the importance of learning. Schools need bright, creative, passionate, personable, highly invested teachers. This principal did not have those dimensions. He might have been more comfortable as a university professor of philosophy, educational foundations, or classical literature. The portrait here evokes a gray memory for me—amid positive memories of that lively teacher culture. Perhaps he relived his elementary and secondary school years daily in that school, feeling like an outsider within the school culture.

Across the individual lifespan, development does not stop. He was at mid-life when he was my school leader. I wonder whether he shifted direction later.

Their Gift

She rarely feels betrayed,
attacked, rejected, ignored,
frightened, panicked, anxious,
but can certainly feel passion
in meaningful enterprise,
sadness over injustices,
frustration about effects
of political manipulation,
anger when someone seems
to question her integrity—
in fact, that is the ungluing,
she says.

She wonders about nature and nurture,
hard-wiring versus context.

There on the farm,
with lightning, hail, and danger,
drought, flood, or blizzard,
accident, illness, or death,
they were steady,
solid, predictable,
poised, problem-solving,
and not anxious,
even in the worst of it.
That was the context
and they were her models.

Their Gift

Psychologists discuss *genotype* (underlying genetic makeup) and *phenotype* (characteristics expressing genetic makeup), the latter a product of both genetic makeup and environmental influences. Temperament (genotype) is likely to be fairly consistent throughout life, reflected in introversion, assertiveness, activity level, inclination toward or away from risk, general intelligence, and anxiety, for example. However, life events, interests, and relationships affect what emerges as personality (phenotype), including intelligence. When I focus momentarily on perfectionism, shyness, or intelligence in workshops and presentations, I refer informally to both temperament and personality. When I attend to anxiety and depression, I often hear questions about both, and we then talk about genes and contexts, too.

Parents and siblings interact complexly, and therefore each child and parent experiences a somewhat different environment and is influenced uniquely by that environment. Family environment and parenting seem to have great influence on personality during childhood. During adolescence, choices and experiences related to interests, relationships, and contexts usually broaden the range of environmental impact.

In this poem, the emphasis is on models—in context. It is not meant to be a value judgment. Parents can influence their children positively in a multitude of ways. In this case, they may have had major parental limitations, but their solidity, in retrospect, was described as the most important gift.

This woman was exploring influences on her low anxiety level, which allowed her to channel her energy into new and interesting domains and contexts without fear and doubt. Certainly, inherited temperament played a role. But she had concluded that context had had great influence. The adult models at home provided extraordinary security, reasonable and appropriate emotional boundaries, and safety in storms, even when thunder during raging downpours shook the farmhouse. Cows had to be milked, sheep fed, eggs gathered, hay baled, oats harvested, and corn picked, regardless of circumstances. No one groused about the work that had to be done. Parental energy was not spent fighting unreasonable fears and worries—or at least that was her perception.

Undoubtedly, their several children did not view their parents similarly. The number of siblings each had at early ages (i.e., the oldest was an only child for a while, there were two until the third child arrived, then three, then four), the personality of each sibling, the ages of their parents when each child was born, the negative and positive life events that occurred in the extended family, and the personalities of available peers were among many factors influencing their view of their childhood and of their parents.

Sad Boy

Pensive parents bring him in,
lanky and serious,
theirs since infancy,
loved gently, deeply,
attentively,
as their own,
vaguely sad now
about school
at 15,
severely gifted,
evident early,
set apart.

Halfway through,
I ask,
"Should we worry about you?"
I hear their eyes snap into focus.
"Yeh," he says, nodding,
extending the syllable with breath.
"How much?"
"Yeh."
And he nods again, faintly smiling.
"Have you thought about hurting yourself?"
"Ya."
More punctuation
and less breath, this time.
Their posture is now straight,
eyes wide,
mouths open.
No words emerge.
I excuse myself
to get a no-suicide contract,
and they are all in tears
when I return.

Sad Boy

This session had a positive outcome. Some of the boy's carefully guarded feelings saw daylight, and he continued to talk with his concerned parents during the next week. They returned for a few more sessions, reporting each time that communication had improved again. There was a lot to sort out, and they were doing that. It is not unusual, at his age, to contemplate the adoption. This boy loved his parents and had no complaints about them, and he hadn't wanted to distress or disappoint them with his concerns. That made sense, we said.

It is not odd for teens to put parents at arm's length. However, sensitive gifted kids may view even feelings of doubt and distress as unfairly challenging their parents. Maybe this boy's sensitivities contributed to his perception that his feelings made him "ungrateful." Pertinent to this, one of my professors once said that it's more difficult for a teen to differentiate from high-functioning parents than to separate from low-functioning parents. He connected that point to families of gifted kids—at least those typically identified. When parents are neglectful or abusive, when they employ inappropriate and ineffective coping strategies to the detriment of others in the family, when their messages are largely negative and critical, and when family leadership is weak, it is not surprising when a child wants to be *unlike* the parents. Distinguishing oneself from "good parents" is more difficult. How does a good child do that?

This sad boy was struggling with identity and wondering about his biological parents and what they had bequeathed him genetically. His sense of differentness socially and cognitively as a highly gifted sophomore had created internal and external dis-ease. The more complex the feelings, the more he felt a need to "stuff them." The more locks he put on the closet, the more intense the feelings, and the more the emotional clutter accumulated. It was hard to sort it out. Counseling was "spring cleaning."

I'm glad that the parents chose an objective stranger with knowledge about giftedness. When I asked, the boy said he knew why they had come. It must have been frightening for his parents to broach the subject of counseling with him. But they had, and he talked readily in sessions. All three of them came back each week with more ease with the process. Each time, we talked more and more about social concerns and did some "solution work." They did the work. This sad boy's demeanor and loss of energy had brought them in. His parents were paying attention. He felt, he talked, his feelings were validated, he received credible feedback, and he moved ahead in his complex development.

Many Kinds

I saw the pained complexity
in brother and cousin,
who had the extreme-IQ kind,
compensated for my own,
because I also had the social kind,
felt the gravitational pull
of kindred spirits,
who were the spatial
and musical kinds,
recognized
the mechanical kind,
loved the aesthetics
of the physical kind,
raised two
with different kinds,
taught those of many kinds,
and felt
in the gut
how they were not seen.
The complexity
defies the stereotypes.

Many Kinds

Each of the portraits in this book reflects at least a few dimensions of social, emotional, and cognitive complexity. As a counselor, if I reflect to students in a school or clients in an agency that they are "wonderfully complex," that their thoughts, feelings, and behaviors are "probably complicated," or that their most troubling life experiences have given them "rich texture," I mean what I say—but I wait until I have enough credibility to say it, based on observation and interaction. Invariably, those words resonate, and their faces reflect a sense of validation. I have indeed been around amazing complexity over several decades, including during my childhood and adolescence. I believe that complexity should be affirmed.

I often use a "13 Intelligences" activity with children, adolescents, and graduate students. This activity works well, regardless of age. We stand in a circle, and I toss to the floor large cartoons representing various strengths. Then I ask participants to name three that they have and one that they definitely don't have. The 13 include a few more than Howard Gardner describes in his multiple intelligences work, such as "strong in life, no matter what," "creative ideas," "insightful," and "common sense," and we often have interesting conversations related to those in particular. The purpose of the activity is to point out narrow "valuing," to celebrate strengths that often do not receive attention, to provide an opportunity for self-affirmation, to be reminded that everyone has limitations, and to allow participants to perhaps find common ground.

One year, when teaching a class of gifted middle school kids, I included a weekly small-group discussion and some speakers, career panels, and creative projects. Because there had been some hints of arrogance and entitlement, I decided to counter this with a field trip to the auto mechanics area at a local high school. After listening to the head teacher explain the complexity of new digital systems, and later watching mechanically adept students work on engines and brakes for a while, they returned to class with new respect for mechanical intelligence, which we had talked about earlier in class. When we did the "13 Intelligences" activity the next day, they were quite forthcoming, including about their limitations, which frequently were mechanical. They understood when I told them I wanted a gifted mechanic when my car or mower motor or household system needed help.

I mention this experience to reflect what I hope this volume of poetic portraits conveys—that "gifted" comes in many kinds of packages, that giftedness can be both asset and burden, that gifted individuals are continually developing and changing, and that there is always (yes, always) more complexity in gifted persons than is probably assumed from the outside. Educators and parents should not make assumptions based on one developmental stage. Finding ways to validate these realities may help sensitive, quietly or overtly intense, and very human individuals feel understood and supported.

Index by Theme

Achievers
Caught Off Guard, 8
Cause and Effect, 16
Eating Disorder, 26
He Couldn't Wait, 52
He Has Edges, 44
High Achiever, 10
Laughing about the Letter, 100
The Nicest Girl in School, 74
The Parent, 32
Seven-Year-Old, 106
Victim, 28
Warm Eyes, 38
When Kennedy Died, 90
When the Advocate Died, 68
Wounded, 70
The Writing on the Wall, 20
Yearbook Photographer, 60

Adult Gifted
Explanation, 96
Laughing about the Letter, 100
Mentor Teacher, 98
A Place with Color, 104
Sasha and I, 116
Small-Town Principal, 122
A Teacher Running, 102
Whatever, 94

Anger
Broken Yardstick, 88
He Has Edges, 44
Hunk, 46
Only by Grace, 62
Persistence, 50

Artistic Talent
Cause and Effect, 16
Not a Good Fit, 6
The Recommendation, 12
Wounded, 70
Yearbook Photographer, 60

Asynchronous Development
Awake at Night, 86
The Credit, 58
Seven-Year-Old, 106
Way Off the Charts, 110

Camouflage
Eighth Grader, 42
He Has Edges, 44
The Nicest Girl in School, 74
Surprised, 112

College and Career
Cause and Effect, 16
He Couldn't Wait, 52
A Memorable Experience, 18
Not a Good Fit, 6
Optimal Range, 120
The Recommendation, 12
The Writing on the Wall, 20
Yearbook Photographer, 60

Depression and Suicide
Grief in the Queue, 108
A Memorable Experience, 18
The Parent, 32
Sad Boy, 126
Trying to Fix Himself, 66
When the Advocate Died, 68

The Writing on the Wall, 20
Yearbook Photographer, 60

Development
About Junior High, 64
At the Workshop, 118
Bonsai Tree, 84
Brian and Christi, 72
Eighth Grader, 42
He Couldn't Wait, 52
Hunk, 46
Not a Good Fit, 6
Only by Grace, 62
Persistence, 50
Presentation by Dr. A, 82
Revenge of the Nerds, 92
Sad Boy, 126
Seven-Year-Old, 106
Surprised, 112
Sweaty, 56
Their Gift, 124
Three Boys, 34
Underachievers, 78
Warm Eyes, 38
Whatever, 94
When the Advocate Died, 68
Wounded, 70
The Writing on the Wall, 20
Yearbook Photographer, 60

Eating Disorder
Eating Disorder, 26

Family Problems
Cause and Effect, 16
He Couldn't Wait, 52
The Nicest Girl in School, 74
The Parent, 32
Persistence, 50
Prisoner of Love, 114
Spoiled, 14
Trying to Fix Himself, 66
Victim, 28
Whatever, 94
When the Advocate Died, 68

Grief and Loss
Grief in the Queue, 108
Persistence, 50
Whatever, 94
When Kennedy Died, 90
When the Advocate Died, 68

Identification
Gifted, 4

Insomnia
Awake at Night, 86
Victim, 28

Introversion
Cause and Effect, 16
Eating Disorder, 26
Persistence, 50
To Hear Better, 40
The Writer, 30

Multiple Intelligences
Many Kinds, 128

Parentification
The Nicest Girl in School, 74
The Parent, 32

Perfectionism
Cause and Effect, 16
High Achiever, 10
The Recommendation, 12
Seven-Year-Old, 106

Profoundly Gifted
Sad Boy, 126
Way Off the Charts, 110
When the Advocate Died, 68

Sensitivity, Intensity, Overexcitability
Achievers, 80
Awake at Night, 86
Common Denominators, 48
The Credit, 58
Guilty, 76

He Couldn't Wait, 52
He Has Edges, 44
High Achiever, 10
Only By Grace, 62
The Parent, 32
Persistence, 50
The Recommendation, 12
Sad Boy, 126
Seven-Year-Old, 106
Spoiled, 14
Three Boys, 34
To Hear Better, 40
Warm Eyes, 38
When the Advocate Died, 68
Wounded, 70
The Writer, 30

Sexual Orientation
Wounded, 70

Stress
Achievers, 80
Awake at Night, 86
Cause and Effect, 16
Common Denominators, 48
Eating Disorder, 26
High Achiever, 10
Hunk, 46
The Nicest Girl in School, 74

Substance Use/Abuse
Explanation, 96
He Couldn't Wait, 52
Only By Grace, 62
Wounded, 70
The Writing on the Wall, 20

Twice Exceptionality
Poor Speller, 54
Warm Eyes, 38

Underachievers
Bonsai Tree, 84
Broken Yardstick, 88
The Credit, 58
Eighth Grader, 42
From A to Z, 24
Goosebumps, 36
Grief in the Queue, 108
Hunk, 46
In the Resistance, 22
A Memorable Experience, 18
Only by Grace, 62
Persistence, 50
Poor Speller, 54
The Recommendation, 12
Revenge of the Nerds, 92
Sweaty, 56
Three Boys, 34
To Hear Better, 40
Underachievers, 78
Whatever, 94

About the Author

Jean Sunde Peterson, Ph.D., is a professor in the Department of Educational Studies at Purdue University, where she directs the School Counseling program. In her first career, she was a high school English and foreign language classroom teacher and received a state Teacher of the Year Award. Later, she created a multi-option gifted education program in a large high school and directed a summer foreign language day camp for children.

Working with small groups of gifted teens for several years inspired her to pursue a doctorate in counselor education at The University of Iowa. On fellowship there, she did clinical work and consulting for the Belin-Blank Center for Gifted Education and applied her group model to gifted students at area schools. Her total of more than 1,300 group sessions led to the research agenda which has guided her second career as a counselor educator.

Reflecting her interests in child and adolescent development and in clinical and educational work with gifted youth, Dr. Peterson has written or co-authored more than 80 books, journal articles, and invited textbook chapters, contributing to both school counseling and gifted education literature and often bridging the two fields. Among her seven books are *The Essential Guide for Talking with Gifted Teens*; *Models of Counseling Gifted Children, Adolescents, and Young Adults*; and *Portrait and Model of a School Counselor*.

Dr. Peterson has won numerous awards in teaching, scholarship, and service at Purdue University and several national research awards, and she often presents keynote and other conference sessions related to her areas of expertise. She is a licensed mental health counselor and a National Certified Counselor, with plans to return to clinical work with gifted children and adolescents and their families in retirement.